FIRST 50 SONGS

YOU SHOULD PLAY ON MOUNTAIN DULCIMER

T0057228

Arranged by Steven B. Eulberg

ISBN 978-1-7051-2666-0

HAL•LEONARD®

Visit Hal Leonard Online at
www.halleonard.com

World headquarters, contact:
Hal Leonard
7777 West Bluemound Road
Milwaukee, WI 53213
Email: info@halleonard.com

In Europe, contact:
Hal Leonard Europe Limited
42 Wigmore Street
Marylebone, London, W1U 2RN
Email: info@halleonardeurope.com

In Australia, contact:
Hal Leonard Australia Pty. Ltd.
4 Lentara Court
Cheltenham, Victoria, 3192 Australia
Email: info@halleonard.com.au

CONTENTS

*Denotes a song that requires 1+ fret

Introduction

The arrangements of popular songs in this book are tailored to the mountain dulcimer and will give you the opportunity to study rhythms, tempos, harmonies, and song forms not normally found in traditional folk and dance music. While arranging these songs, I sought to remain faithful to the source material by including as many signature "hooks," interwoven musical lines, and song-specific chord voicings as possible.

Due to its current popularity among both players and builders, I have assumed the use of fret 6+ (or 6 1/2). A few songs also include fret 1+ (or 1 1/2), and one song uses fret 8+ (or 8 1/2), which is the same note as fret 1+ but an octave higher. Most of these arrangements are presented in 1–5–8 (D–A–d) tuning; a few are presented in 1–5–♭7 (D–A–C).

These arrangements can be played fingerstyle or with a pick. If you choose to use a pick, keep in mind that some songs will occasionally require a hybrid-picking approach: playing one note with the pick and another note with a finger at the same time. Left-hand articulations (things like slides, hammer-ons and pull-offs, and bends) are notated in both the standard notation and tablature.

Before jumping into an arrangement, take some time to get familiar with the song's structure. Scan through it, looking for things like repeat signs, first and second endings, and other markers to help navigate the song.

Each arrangement is designed to be played three ways:

1. **Play the melody** by using only the larger numbers in the tablature.
2. **Play the chordal accompaniment** by following the chord symbols above the staff and the chord diagrams below the song title. Invent a strum pattern based on number of beats per measure (see the time signature at the beginning of the note staff—the top number indicates beats per measure) or listen to the original recordings to find other rhythmic ideas. Use this approach when accompanying a singer or giving the melody line to another instrument.
3. **Play the full chord/melody arrangement** as shown in the standard notation or tablature.

I'm grateful to Ronny Schiff for introducing me to Jeff Schroedl at Hal Leonard, and to Jeff for inviting me to arrange these tunes and for encouraging me to seek out and include important tunes from the jukebox of my life. It has been a joy to work on this project. My thanks go out to Jim Schustedt and the team at Hal Leonard for making this music available to you!

Play on and play with joy.

—**Steve Eulberg** (Boise, 2021)

All I Have to Do Is Dream

Words and Music by Boudleaux Bryant

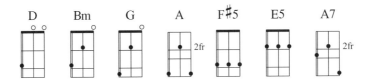

D-A-d tuning
Key: D Major

Intro
Moderately

Dream, ____ dream, dream, dream. ____ Dream, ____

Verse

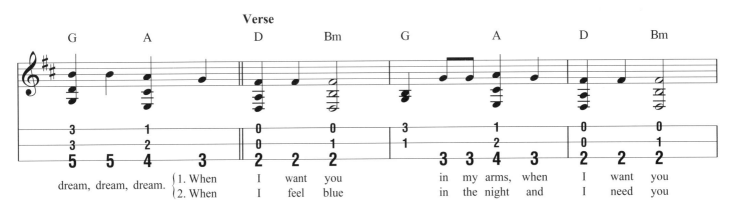

dream, dream, dream.   1. When   I   want   you   in my arms, when   I   want   you
                       2. When   I   feel   blue   in the night and   I   need   you

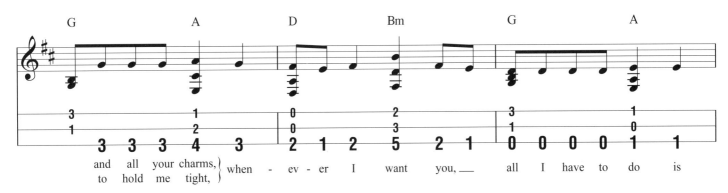

and   all   your charms,   when-ev-er   I   want   you, ____   all   I   have   to do   is
to   hold   me   tight,

1.

2.

dream, ____   dream, dream,   dream. ____   dream.

Bridge

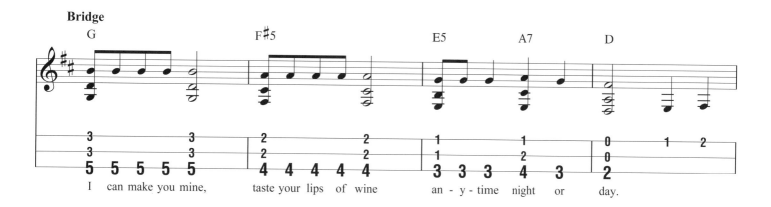

G   **F#5**   **E5**   **A7**   **D**

I can make you mine,   taste your lips of wine   an - y - time night or day.

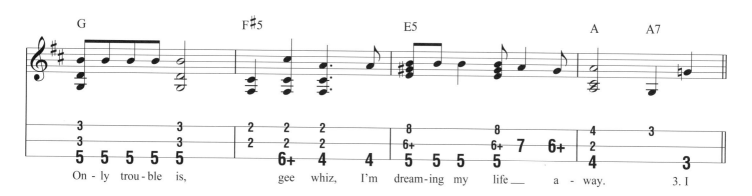

G   **F#5**   **E5**   **A**   **A7**

On - ly trou - ble is,   gee whiz, I'm dream-ing my life ___ a - way.   3. I

Verse

D   **Bm**   **G**   **A**   **D**   **Bm**   **G**   **A**

need you so   that I could die, I love you so   and that is why when -

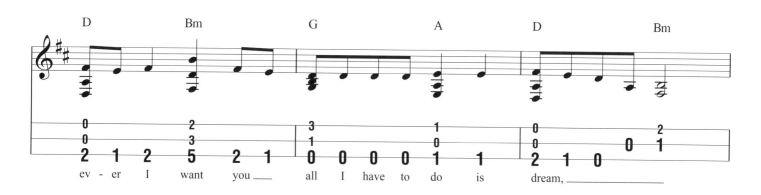

D   **Bm**   **G**   **A**   **D**   **Bm**

ev - er I want you ___ all I have to do is dream, _____

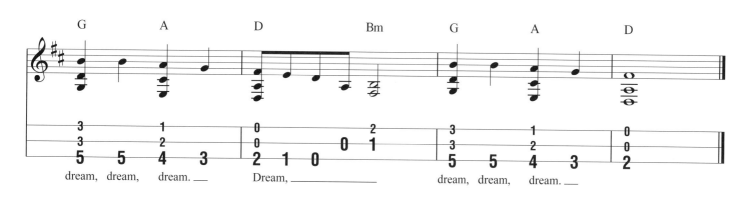

G   **A**   **D**   **Bm**   **G**   **A**   **D**

dream, dream, dream. ___ Dream, _____ dream, dream, dream. ___

All the Pretty Little Horses

Southeastern American Folksong

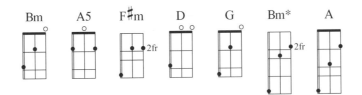

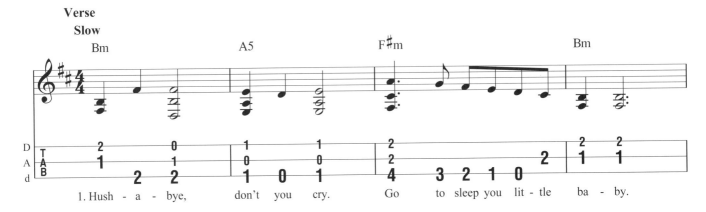

D-A-d tuning
Key: B minor

Verse
Slow

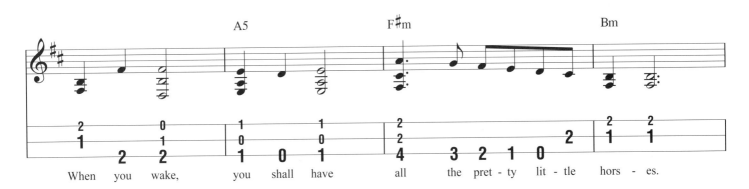

1. Hush - a - bye, don't you cry. Go to sleep you lit - tle ba - by.

When you wake, you shall have all the pret - ty lit - tle hors - es.

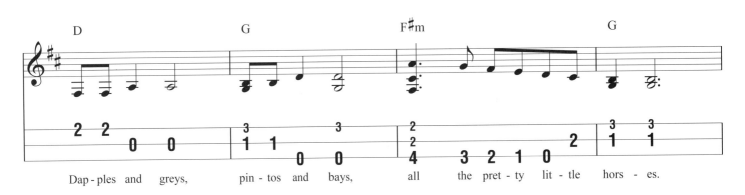

Dap - ples and greys, pin - tos and bays, all the pret - ty lit - tle hors - es.

Hush - a - bye, don't you cry. Go to sleep you lit - tle ba - by.

Desperado

Words and Music by Don Henley and Glenn Frey

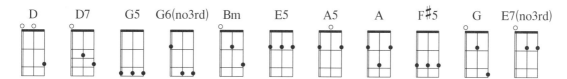

D-A-d tuning
Key: D Major
(Requires 1+ fret)

Intro
Slow

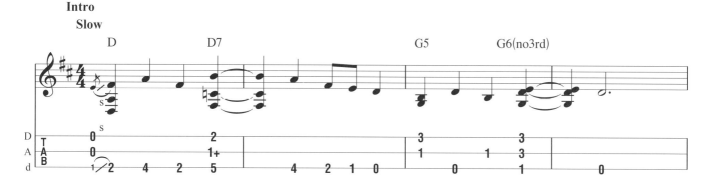

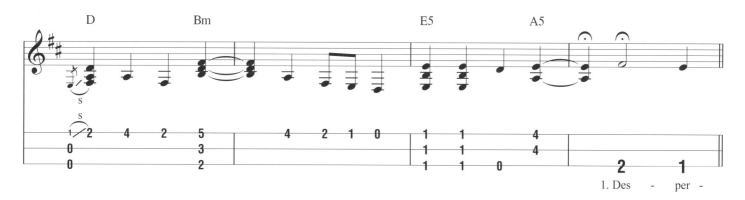

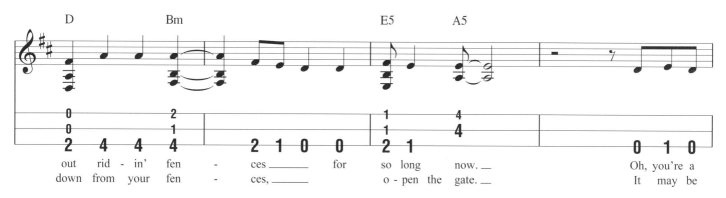

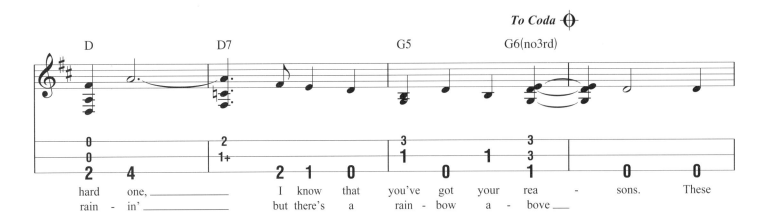

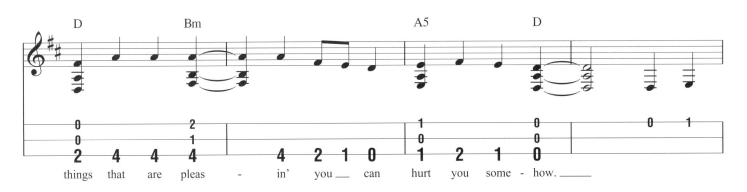

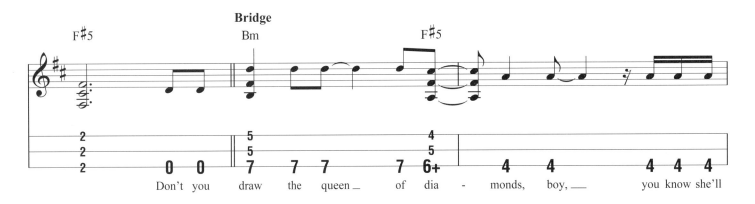

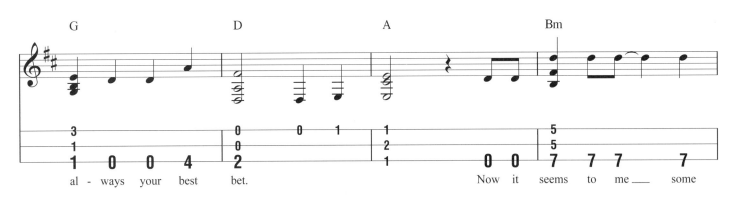

fine   things   have   been   laid   u - pon ___ your   ta - ble, _____   but   you

D.S. al Coda

on - ly   want ___ the   ones   that   you   can't   get.   2. Des - per -

⊕ Coda

___ you.   You   bet - ter   let   some - bod - y   love _____ you.   Let   some - bod - y   love

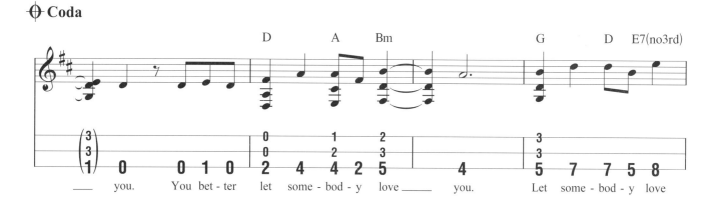

you.   You   bet - ter   let   some - bod - y   love _____   you _____   be - fore   it's   too

Outro

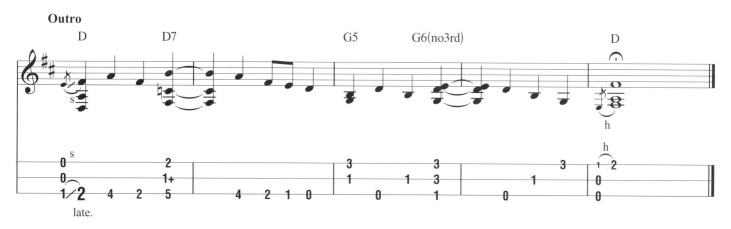

late.

Always on My Mind

Words and Music by Wayne Thompson, Mark James and Johnny Christopher

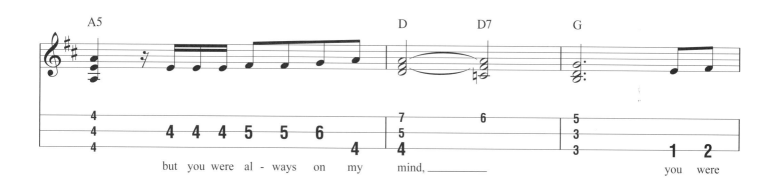

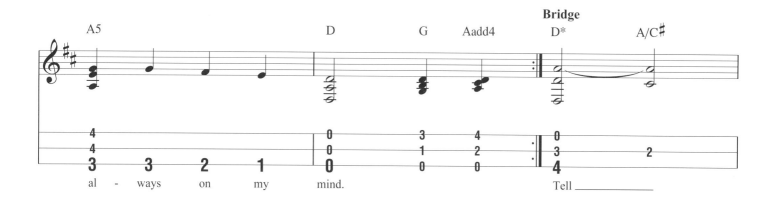

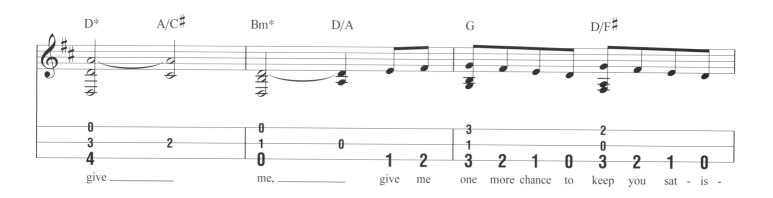

Blowin' in the Wind

Words and Music by Bob Dylan

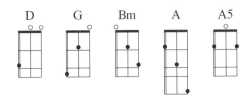

D-A-d tuning
Key: D Major

Verse

Moderately slow

1. How man - y roads must a man walk ___ down be -

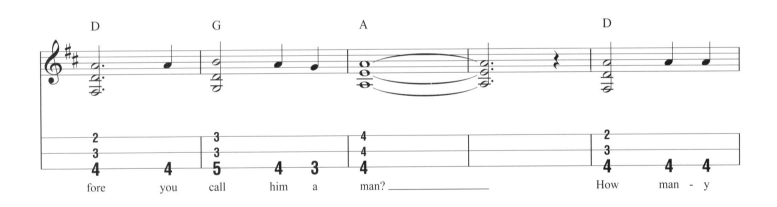

fore you call him a man? ___ How man - y

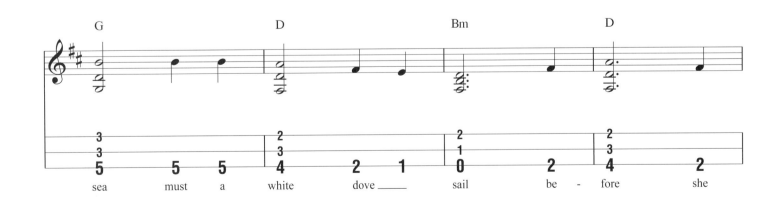

sea must a white dove ___ sail be - fore she

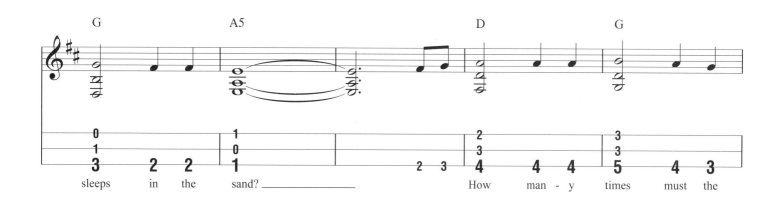

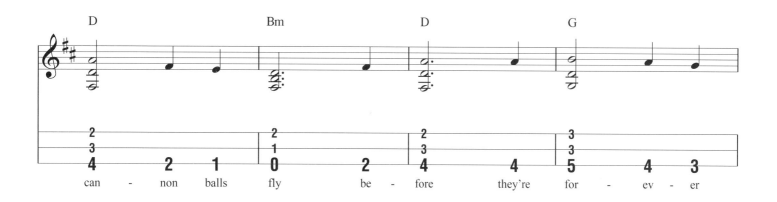

Chorus

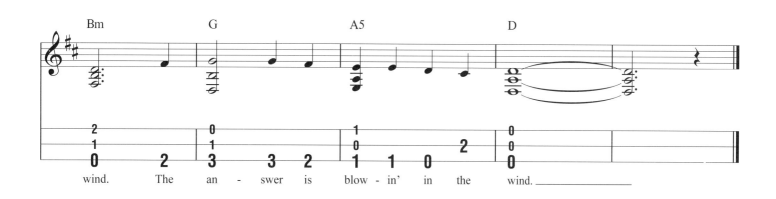

Blue Bayou

Words and Music by Roy Orbison and Joe Melson

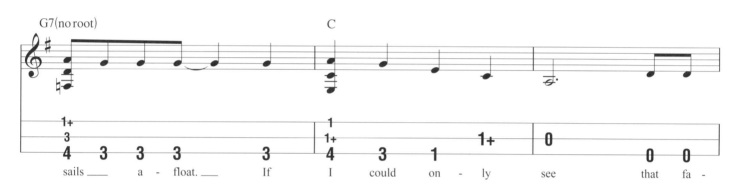

To Coda ⊕   *D.S. al Coda*

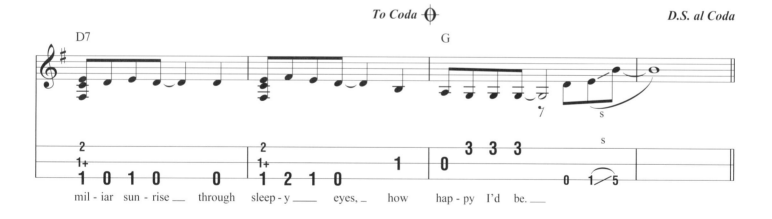

⊕ **Coda**

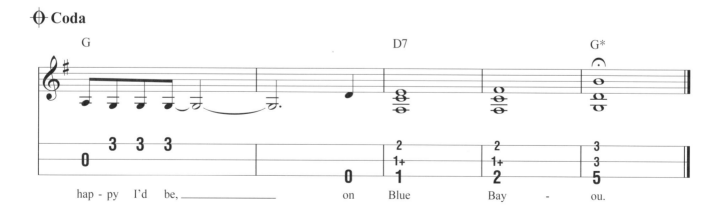

Bridge Over Troubled Water

Words and Music by Paul Simon

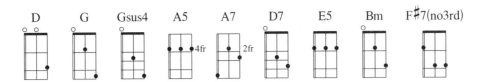

D-A-d tuning
Key: D Major
(Requires 1+ fret for chord diagrams only)

Verse

Slow

Brown Eyed Girl

Words and Music by Van Morrison

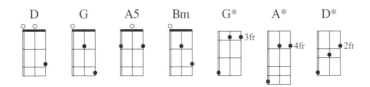

D-A-d tuning
Key: D Major

Intro
Moderately

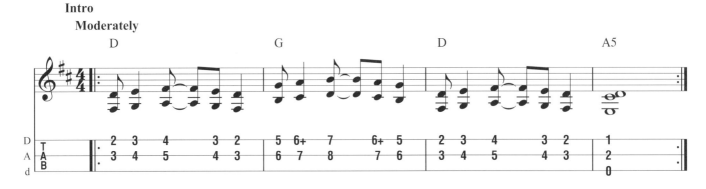

Verse

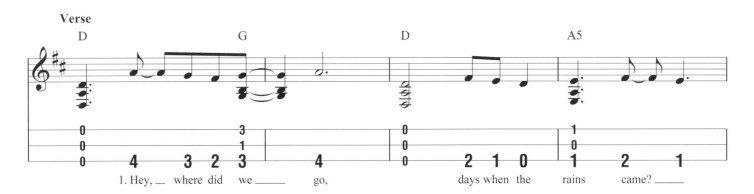

1. Hey, __ where did we ____ go,　　days when the rains came? ____

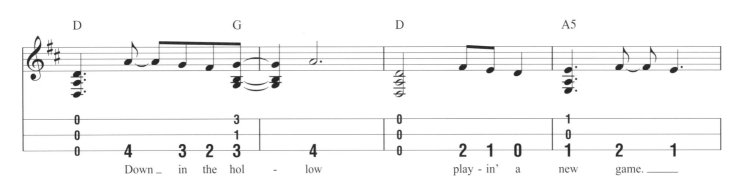

Down __ in the hol - low　　play - in' a new game. ____

Laugh-ing and a - run - nin', hey, __ hey.　Skip-ping and a - jump - in' ____

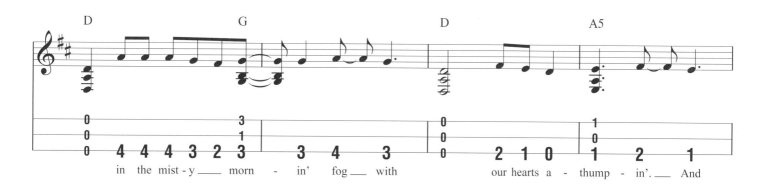

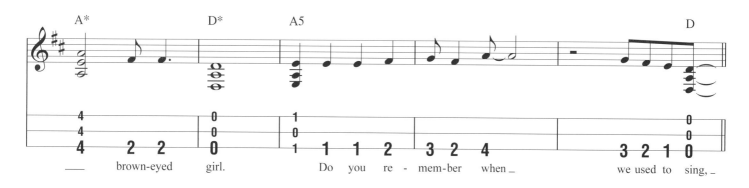

Cat's in the Cradle

Words and Music by Harry Chapin and Sandy Chapin

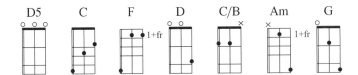

D-A-d tuning
Key: D Major
(Requires 1+ fret)

Intro

Moderately, in 2

Verse

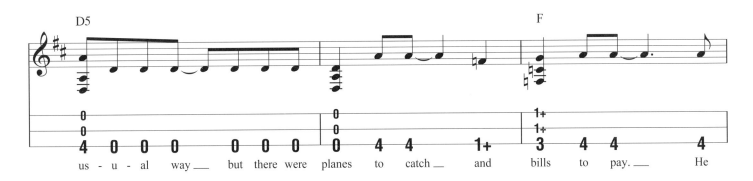

as ___ he grew ___ he'd say, "I'm gon - na be like you, Dad, you

Chorus

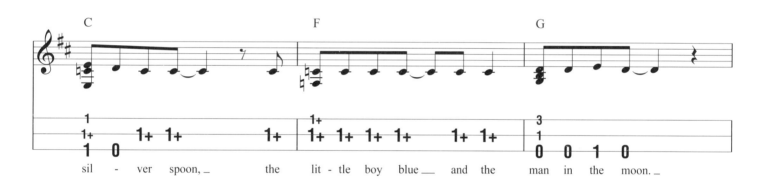

know I'm gon - na be like you." And the cat's in the cra - dle and the

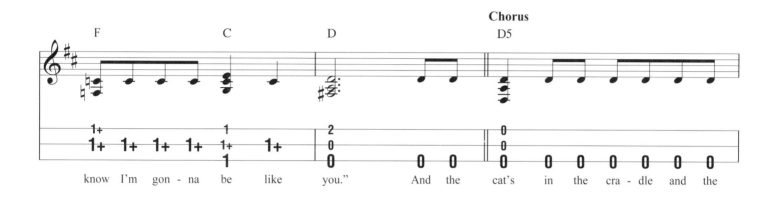

sil - ver spoon, ___ the lit - tle boy blue ___ and the man in the moon. ___

"When you com - in' home, Dad?" "I don't know when, but we'll get to - geth - er

D.C. al Fine

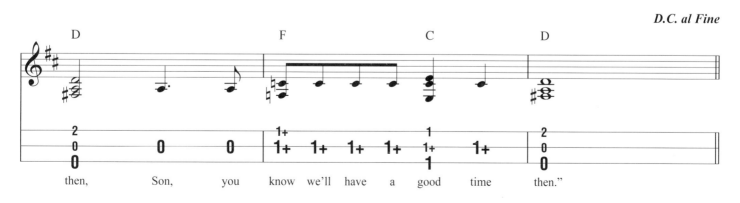

then, Son, you know we'll have a good time then."

Dance with Me

Words and Music by John and Johanna Hall

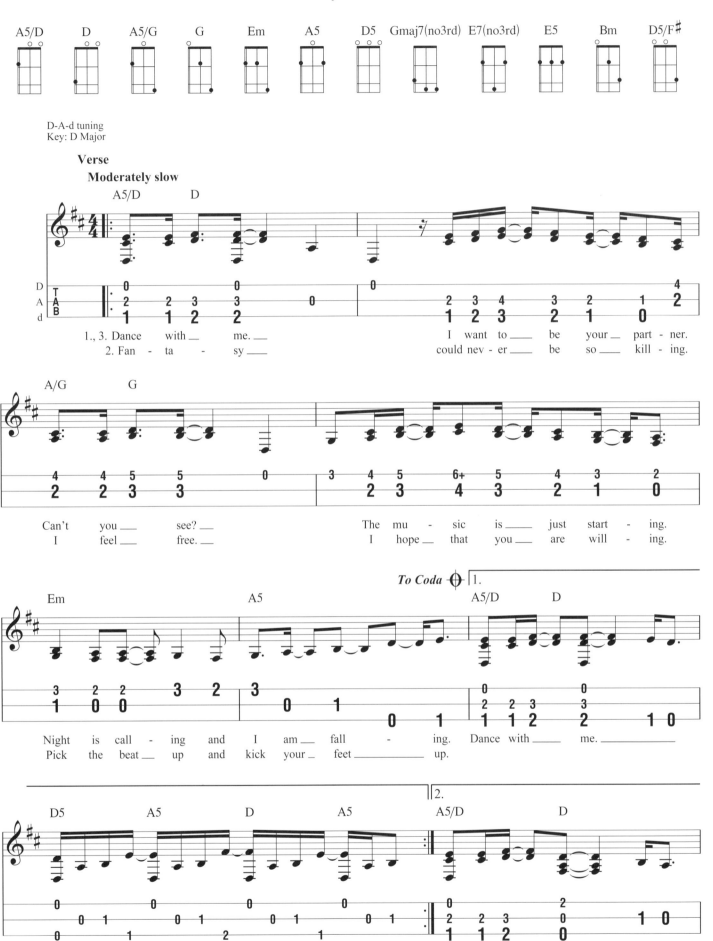

Chorus

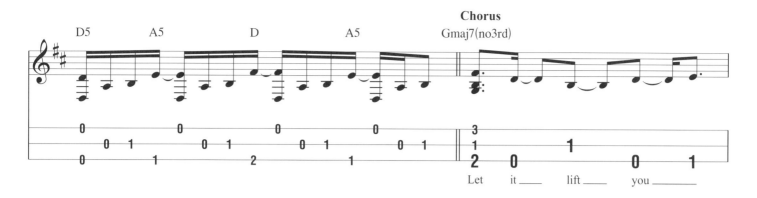

Let it ___ lift ___ you ___

off the ___ ground. ___ Star - ry ___ eyes ___ and love is all ___ a - round ___ us.

D.C. al Coda

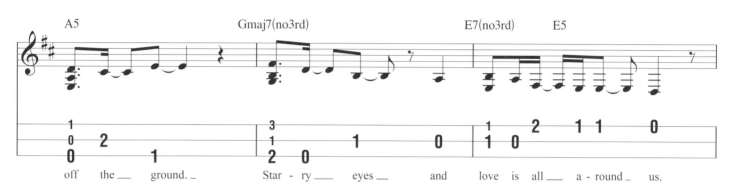

I can take ___ you where ___ you ___ want ___ to go. ___ Oh, ___

 Coda

Outro

Dance with ___ me. ___

†No chord

Dancing Queen

Words and Music by Benny Andersson, Bjorn Ulvaeus and Stig Anderson

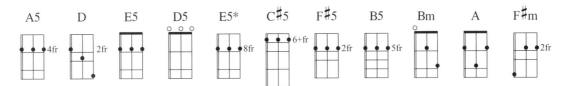

D-A-d tuning
Key: A Major

Intro
Moderately

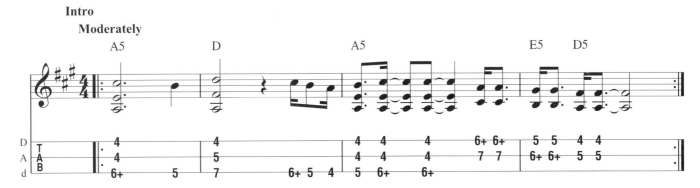

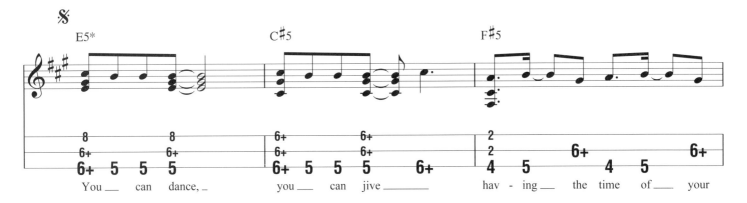

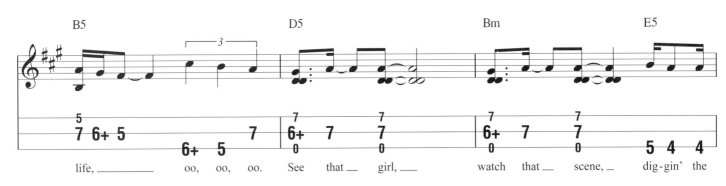

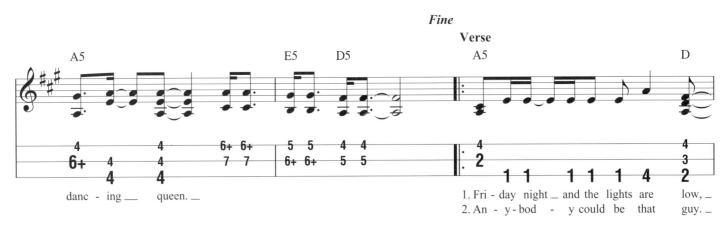

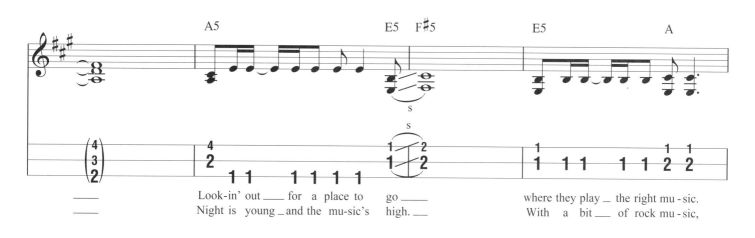

Look-in' out ____ for a place to go ____ where they play __ the right mu-sic.
Night is young __ and the mu-sic's high. __ With a bit __ of rock mu-sic,

Get-tin' in - to the swing, you come to look for a ____ king. __
ev-'ry-thing __ is fine. __ You're in the mood for a ____ dance. __

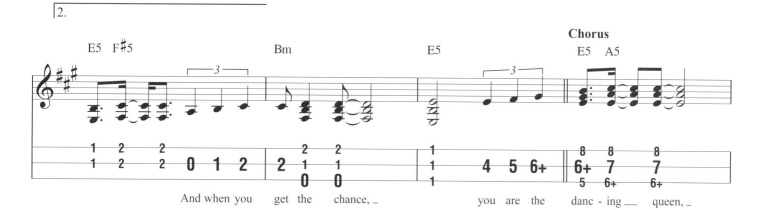

And when you get the chance, _ you are the danc-ing __ queen, _

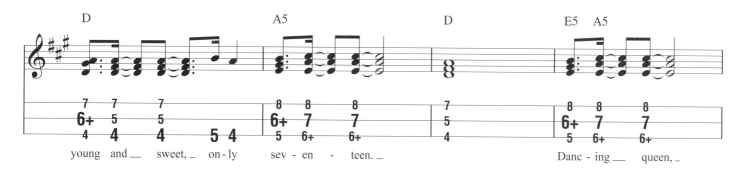

young and __ sweet, _ on-ly sev-en-teen. __ Danc-ing __ queen, _

D.S. al Fine

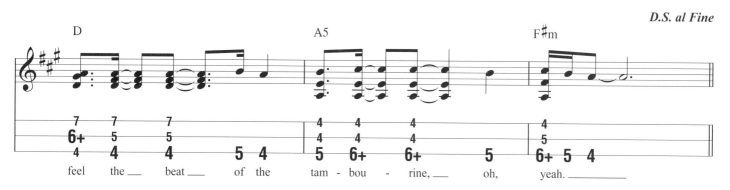

feel the __ beat __ of the tam-bou-rine, __ oh, yeah. _____

(Sittin' On) The Dock of the Bay

Words and Music by Steve Cropper and Otis Redding

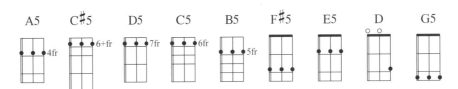

D-A-d tuning
Key: A Major

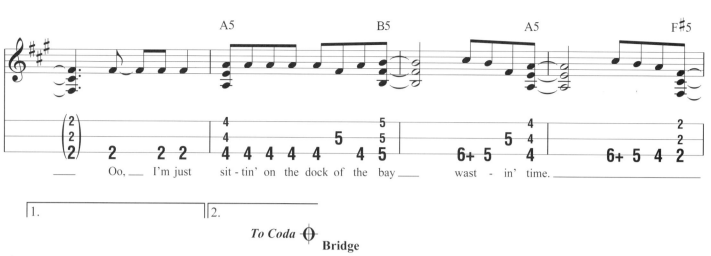

Oo, ___ I'm just sit-tin' on the dock of the bay ___ wast - in' time.

1. 2.

To Coda ⊕
Bridge

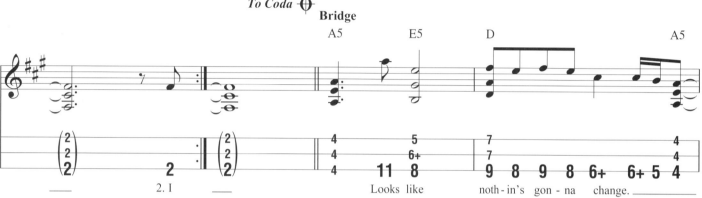

2. I ___ Looks like noth-in's gon-na change. ___

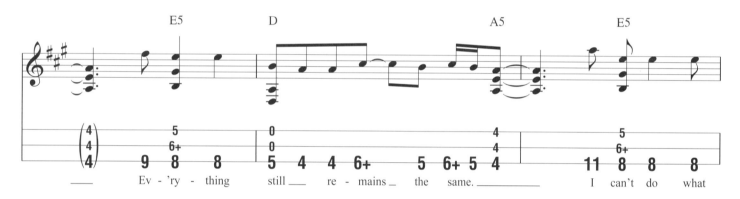

Ev -'ry - thing still ___ re - mains ___ the same. ___ I can't do what

D.S. al Coda
(take 2nd ending)

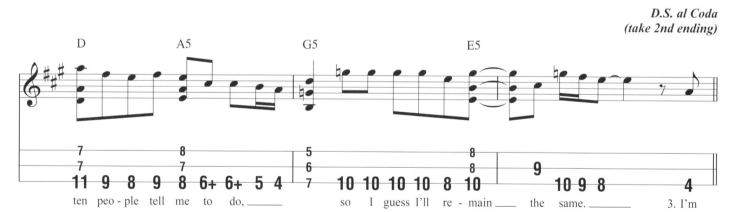

ten peo-ple tell me to do, ___ so I guess I'll re - main ___ the same. ___ 3. I'm

⊕ **Coda**

Outro

Repeat & fade

whistling

29

Fire and Rain

Words and Music by James Taylor

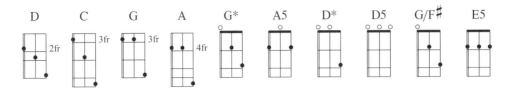

D-A-d tuning
Key: D Major
(Requires 1+ fret)

Verse
Moderately

1. Just yes - ter - day morn - ing, they let me know you were gone. ___

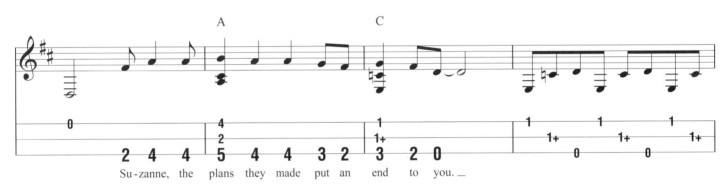

Su - zanne, the plans they made put an end to you. _

Walked out this morn - ing and I wrote down this song. ___

I just can't re - mem - ber who to send it to.

Chorus

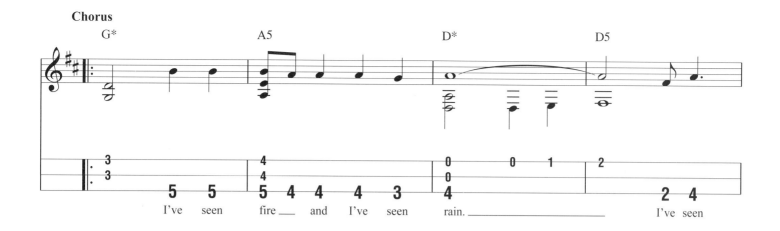

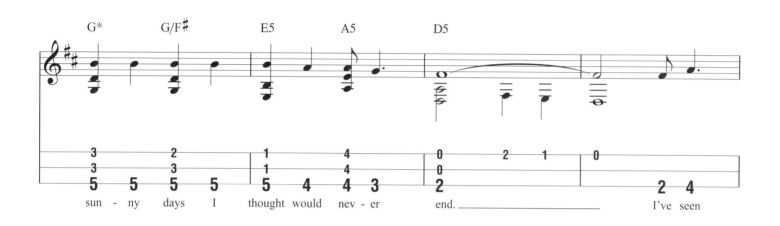

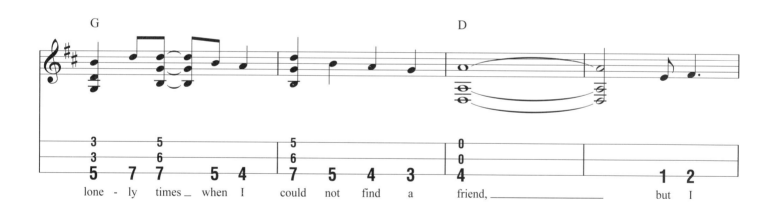

2nd time, Begin fade *Fade out*

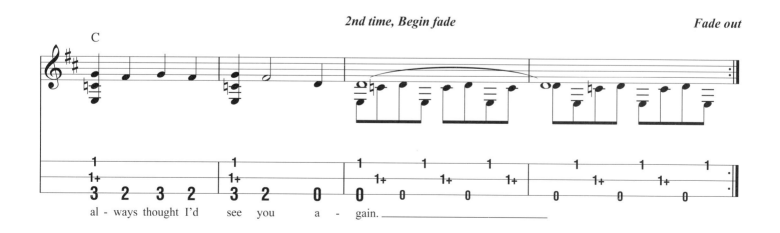

The House of the Rising Sun

Words and Music by Alan Price

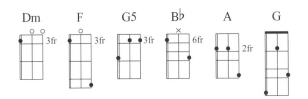

D-A-C tuning
Key: D minor
(Requires 1+ fret)

Verse
Moderately slow

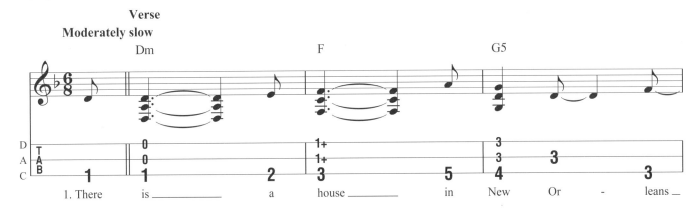

I Can See Clearly Now

Words and Music by Johnny Nash

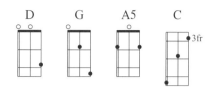

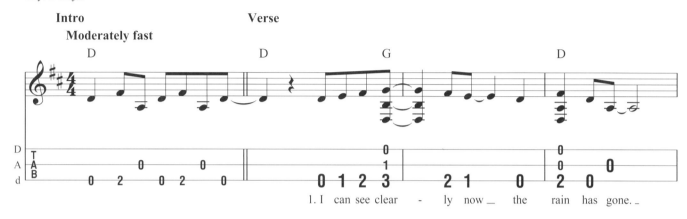

D-A-d tuning
Key: D Major

Intro

Moderately fast

Verse

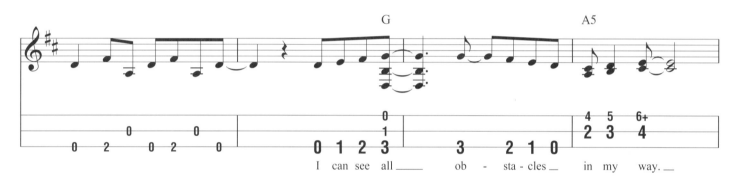

1. I can see clear - ly now _ the rain has gone. _

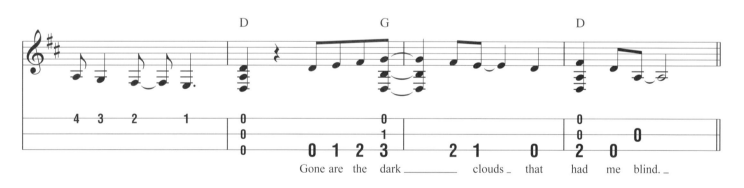

I can see all ___ ob - sta - cles _ in my way. _

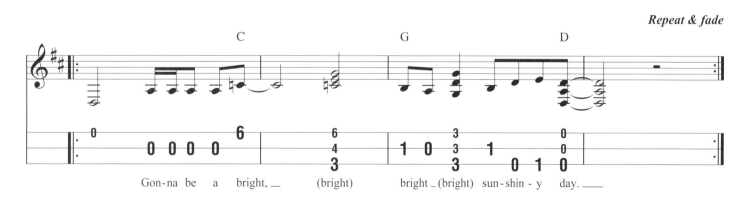

Gone are the dark ___ clouds _ that had me blind. _

Repeat & fade

Gon - na be a bright, _ (bright) bright _ (bright) sun - shin - y day. ___

I Saw the Light

Words and Music by Hank Williams

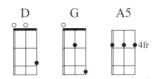

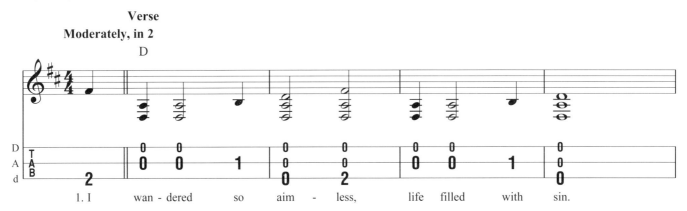

D-A-d tuning
Key: D Major

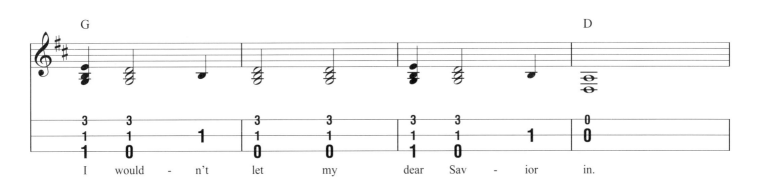

1. I wan - dered so aim - less, life filled with sin.

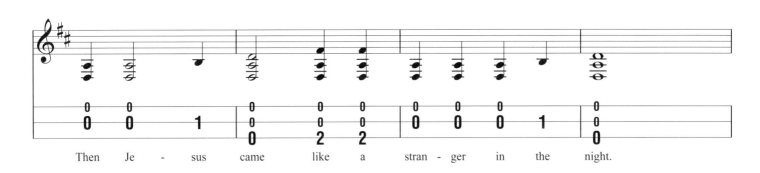

I would - n't let my dear Sav - ior in.

Then Je - sus came like a stran - ger in the night.

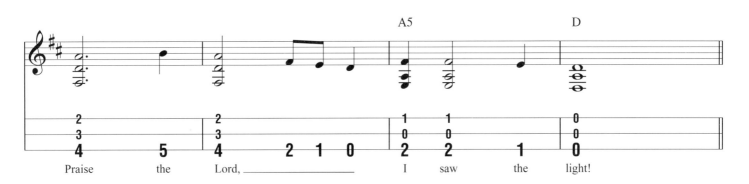

Praise the Lord, _____ I saw the light!

Chorus

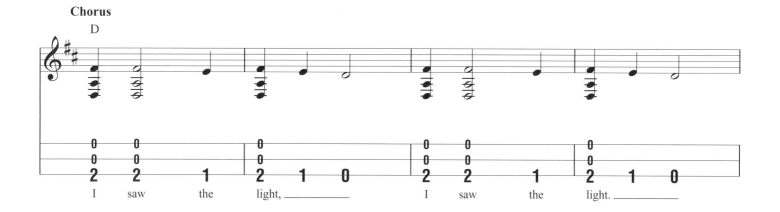

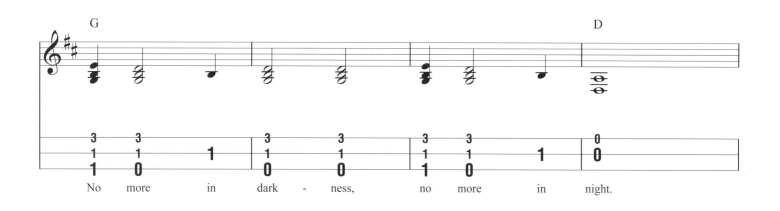

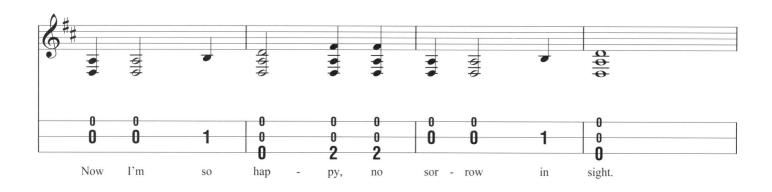

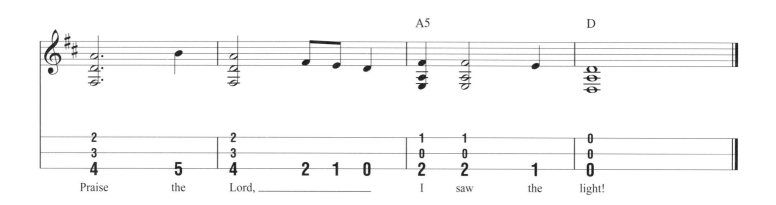

If I Had a Hammer
(The Hammer Song)

Words and Music by Lee Hays and Pete Seeger

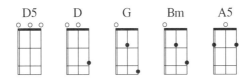

D-A-d tuning
Key: D Major

Verse

Moderately, in 2

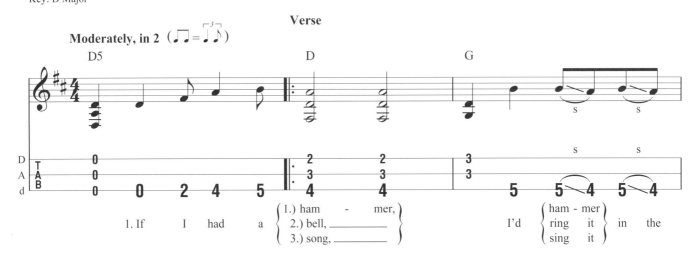

1. If I had a
{ 1.) ham - mer,
  2.) bell, _____
  3.) song, _____ }
I'd { ring it
      sing it } in the

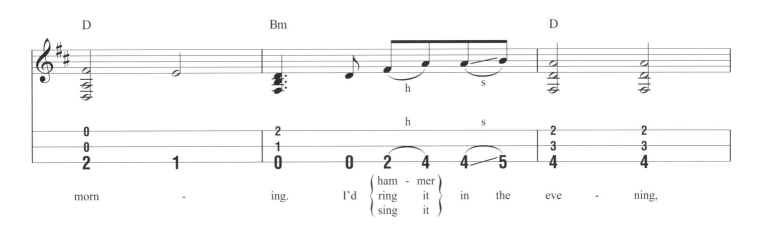

morn - - ing. I'd { ring it
                     sing it } in the eve - ning,

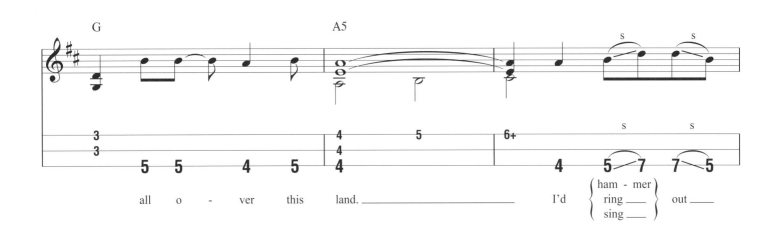

all o - ver this land. _____ I'd { ring ___
                                        sing ___ } out ___

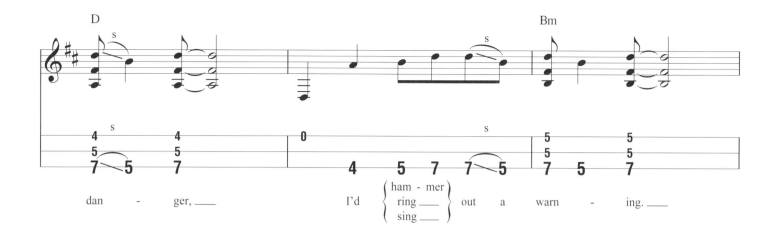

dan - ger, ___ I'd { ham - mer / ring ___ / sing ___ } out a warn - ing. ___

I'd { ham - mer / ring ___ / sing ___ } out the love be - tween my broth - ers and my sis - ters,

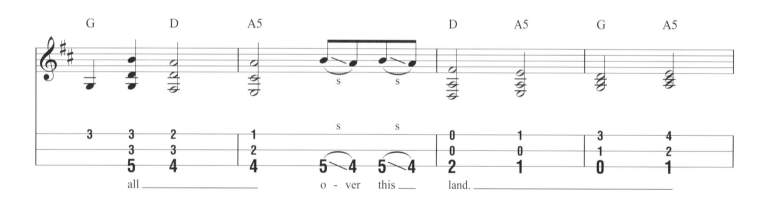

all ___ o - ver this ___ land. ___

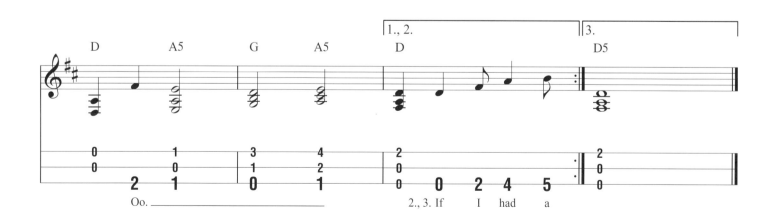

Oo. ___ 2., 3. If I had a

Imagine

Words and Music by John Lennon

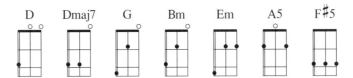

D-A-d tuning
Key: D Major
(Requires 1+ fret)

Verse

Moderately

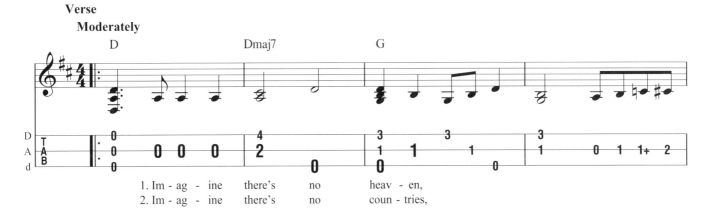

1. Im - ag - ine there's no heav - en,
2. Im - ag - ine there's no coun - tries,

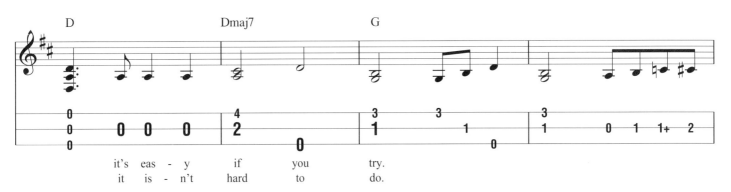

it's eas - y if you try.
it is - n't hard to do.

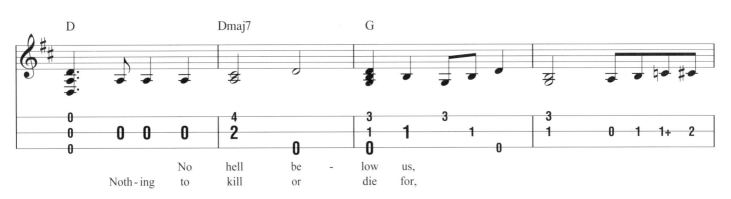

No hell be - low us,
Noth - ing to kill or die for,

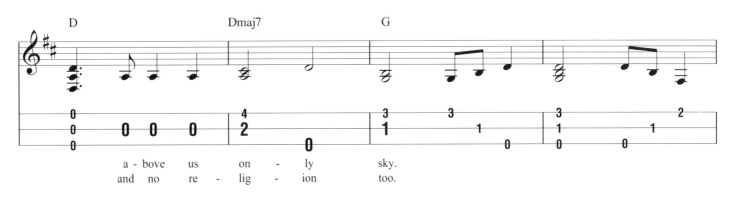

a - bove us on - ly sky.
and no re - lig - ion too.

In My Room

Words and Music by Brian Wilson and Gary Usher

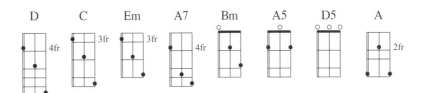

D-A-d tuning
Key: D Major
(Requires 1+ fret)

Verse
Slow

1. There's a world where I can go and
2. In this world, I lock out all my
3. Now it's dark and I'm a - lone, but

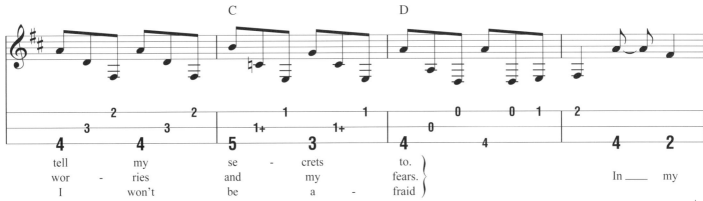

tell my se - crets to.
wor - ries and my fears.
I won't be a - fraid

To Coda ⊕

In ___ my

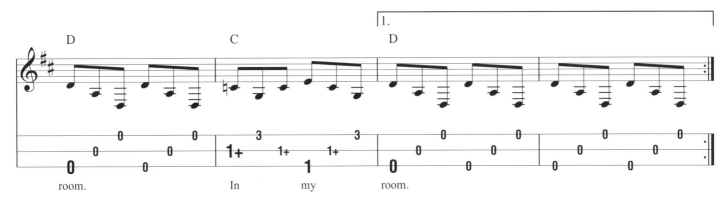

room, in ___ my

room. In my room.

2.

Bridge

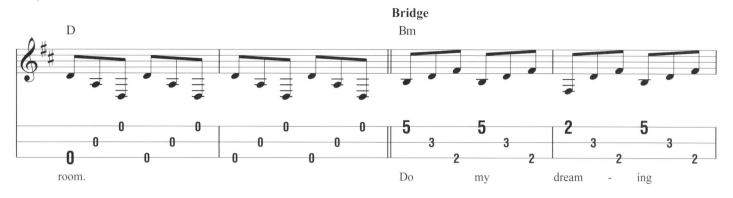

room.　　Do　my　dream - ing

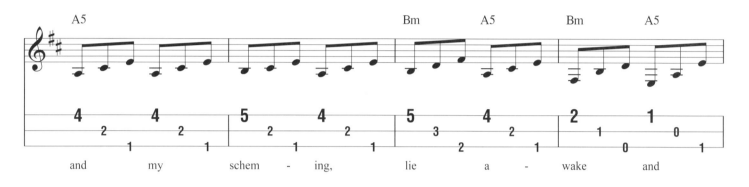

and　　my　　schem - ing,　lie　a - wake　and

pray. _____　　Do　my　cry - ing　and　my

D.C. al Coda

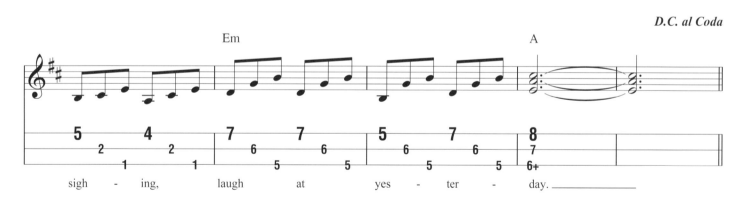

sigh - ing,　laugh　at　yes - ter - day. _____

 Coda

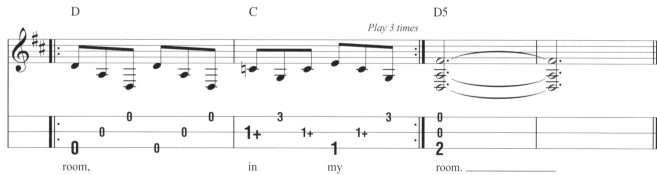

room,　　in　my　　room. _____

Isn't She Lovely

Words and Music by Stevie Wonder

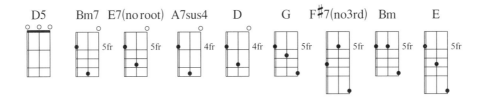

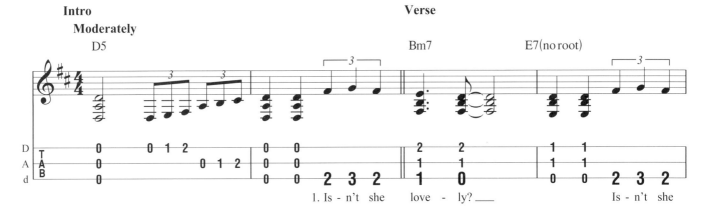

D-A-d tuning
Key: D Major

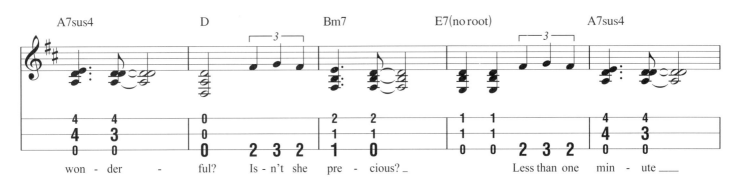

Kansas City

Words and Music by Jerry Leiber and Mike Stoller

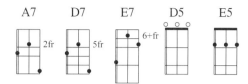

D-A-d tuning
Key: A Major

Verse

Moderately

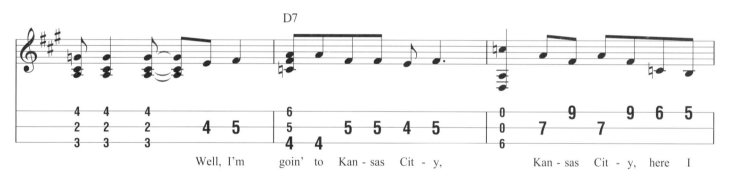

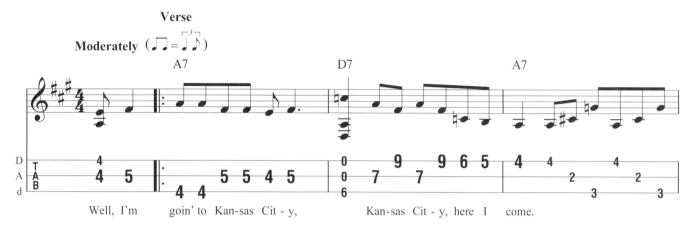

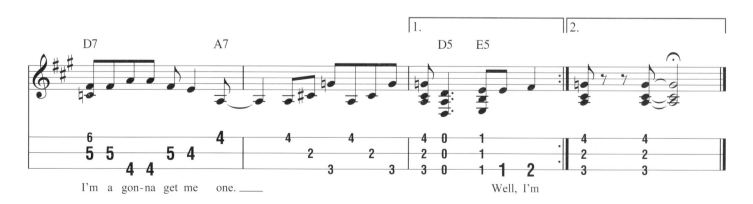

It Had to Be You

Words by Gus Kahn
Music by Isham Jones

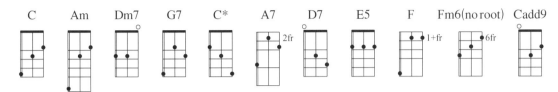

D-A-d tuning
Key: C Major
(Requires 1+ & 8+ frets)

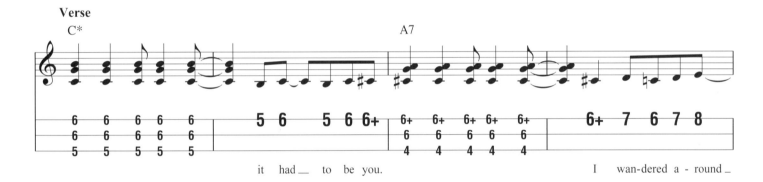

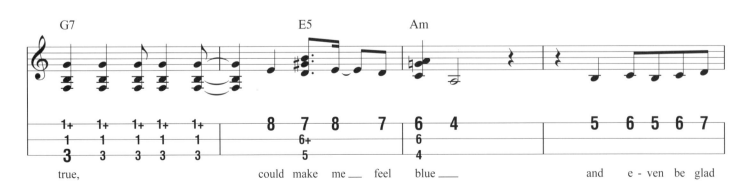

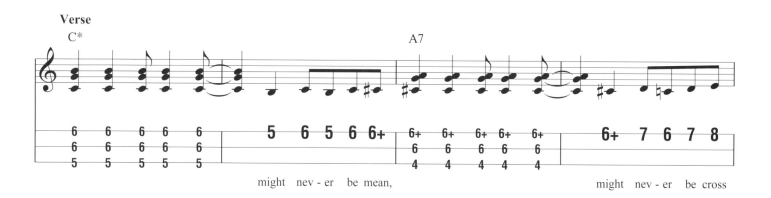

Verse

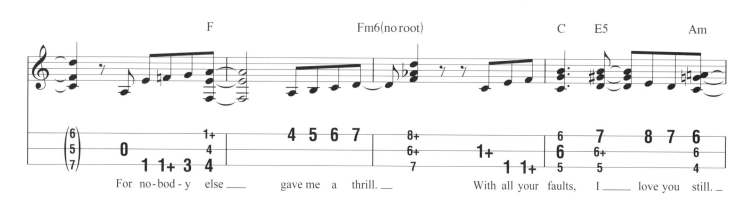

Jolene

Words and Music by Dolly Parton

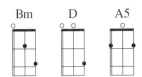

D-A-d tuning
Key: B minor

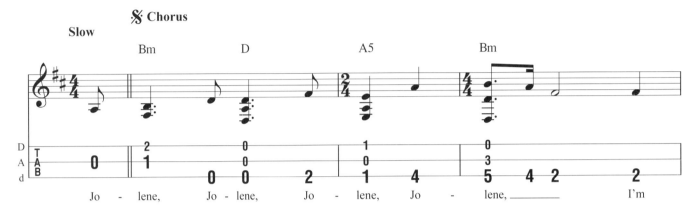

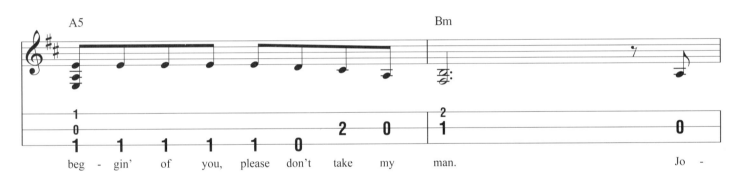

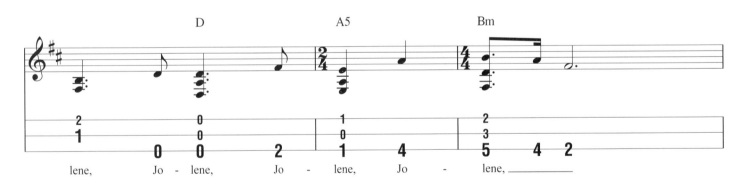

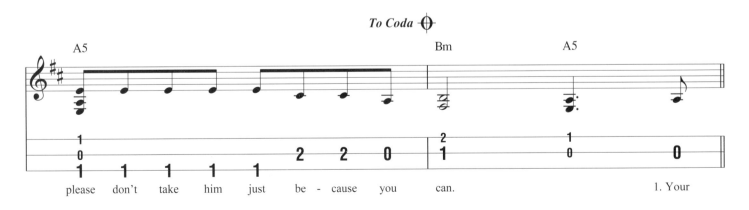

Verse

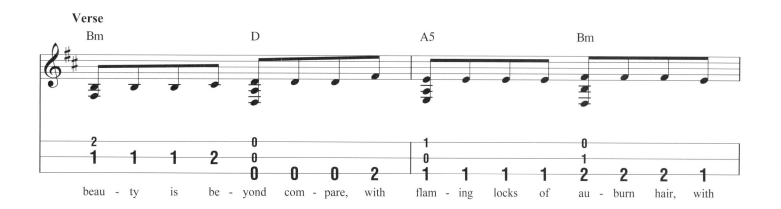

beau-ty is be-yond com-pare, with flam-ing locks of au-burn hair, with

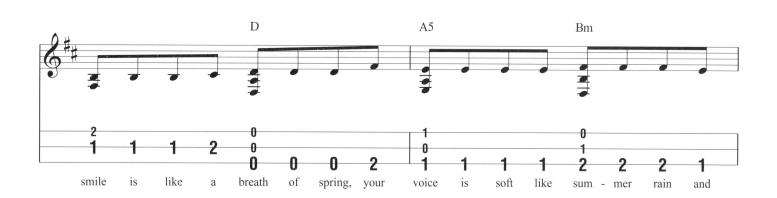

i-v'ry skin and eyes of em'-rald green. Your

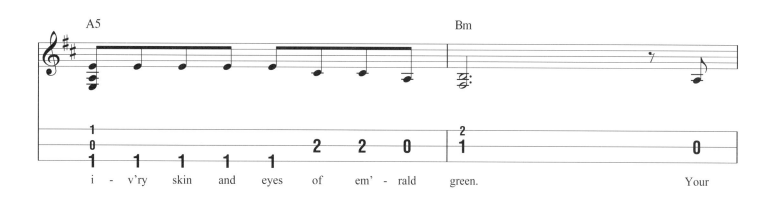

smile is like a breath of spring, your voice is soft like sum-mer rain and

D.S. al Coda   ⊕ **Coda**

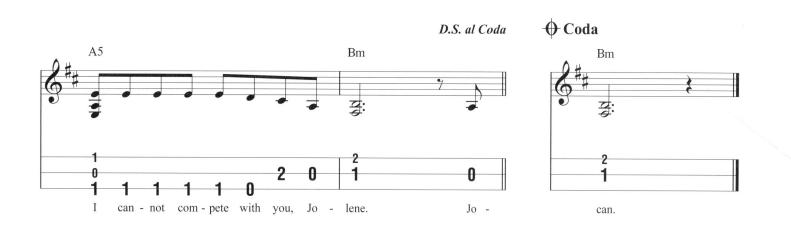

I can-not com-pete with you, Jo-lene. Jo-   can.

Keep on the Sunny Side

Words and Music by A.P. Carter

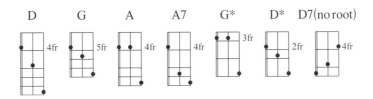

D-A-d tuning
Key: D Major

Verse

Moderately, in 2

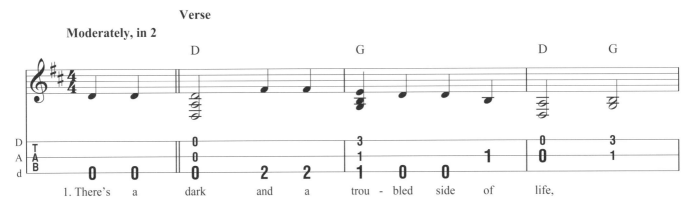

1. There's a dark and a trou - bled side of life,

there's a bright and a sun - ny side too.

Though you meet with the dark - ness and strife, _____

_____ the sun - ny side we al - so may view. _____

48

Chorus

Keep on the sun - ny - side, ___ al - ways on the

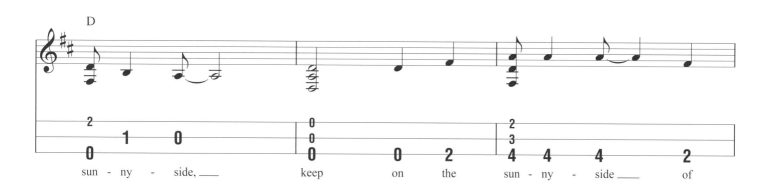

sun - ny - side, ___ keep on the sun - ny - side ___ of

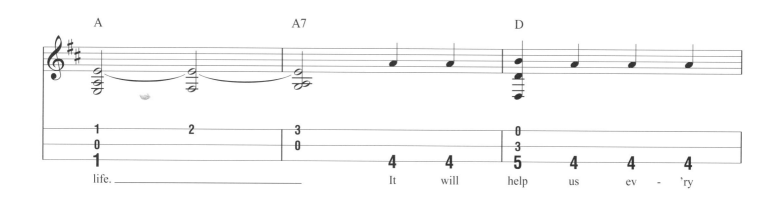

life. _____ It will help us ev - 'ry

day, it will bright - en all the way if we'll

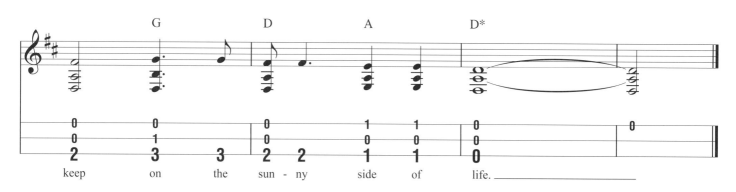

keep on the sun - ny side of life. _____

Kentucky Waltz

Words and Music by Bill Monroe

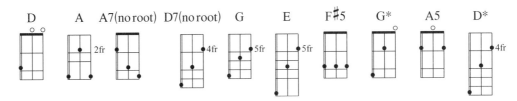

D-A-d tuning
Key: D Major

Verse

Moderately

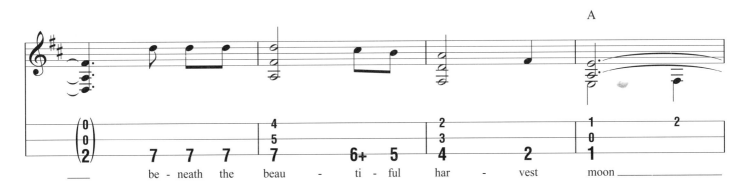

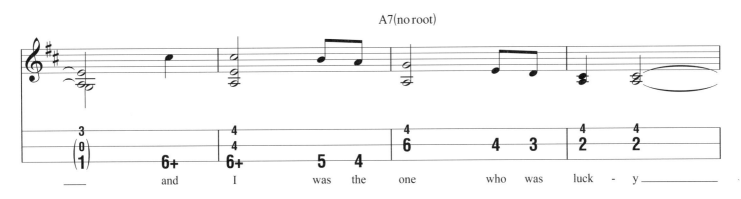

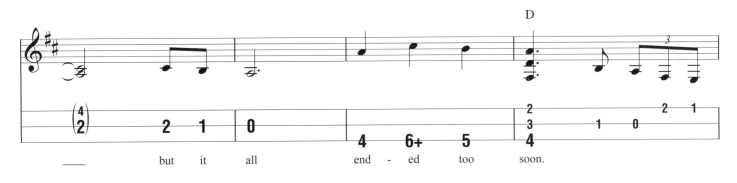

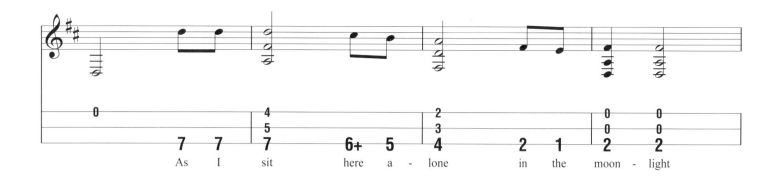

As I sit here a - lone in the moon - light

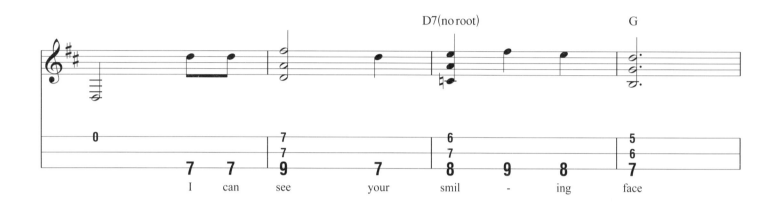

D7(no root)   G

I can see your smil - ing face

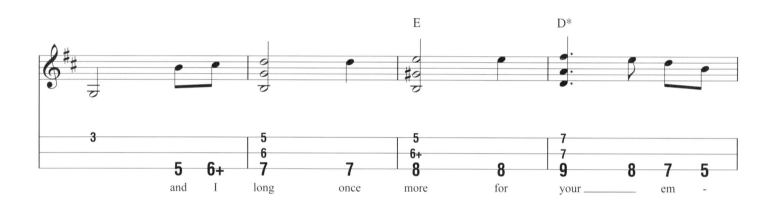

E   D*

and I long once more for your _____ em -

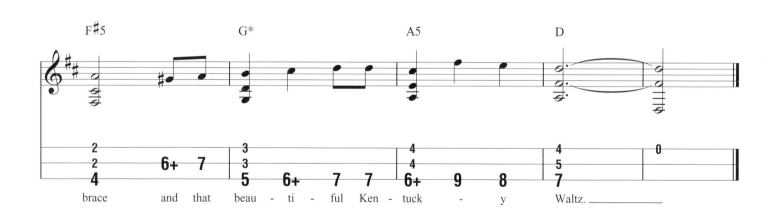

F#5   G*   A5   D

brace and that beau - ti - ful Ken - tuck - y Waltz. _____

Leader of the Band

Words and Music by Dan Fogelberg

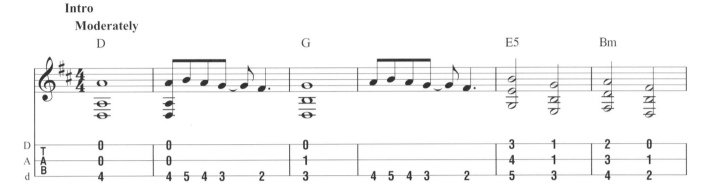

D-A-d tuning
Key: D Major

Intro
Moderately

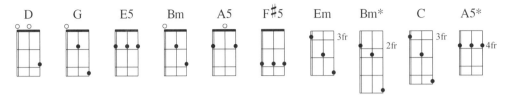

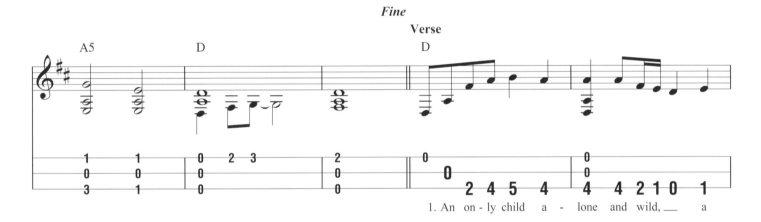

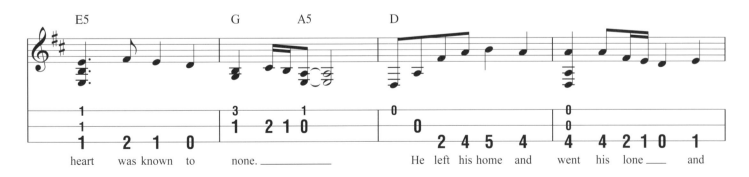

Chorus

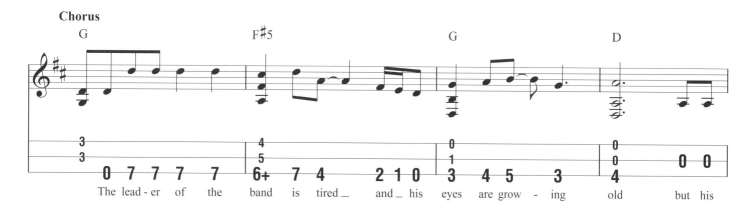

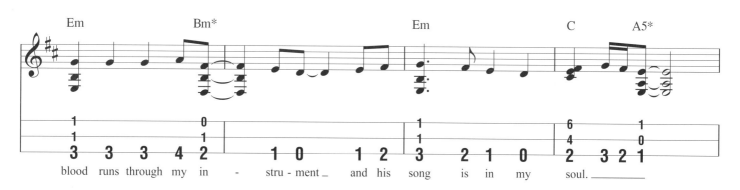

D.C. al Fine

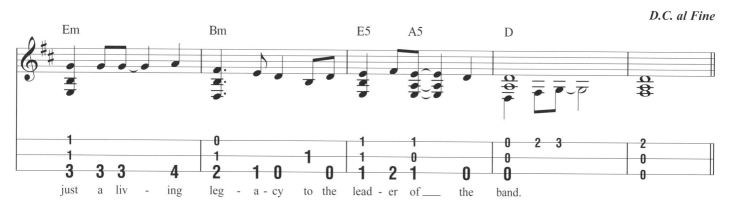

Lean on Me

Words and Music by Bill Withers

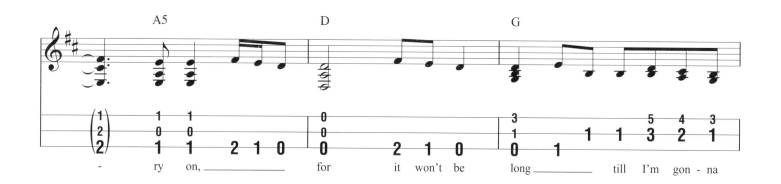

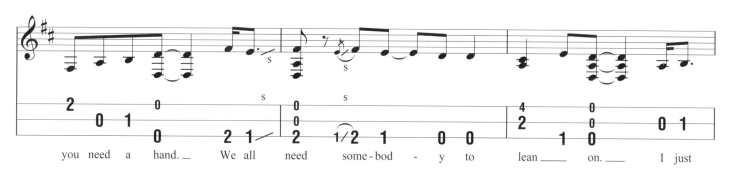

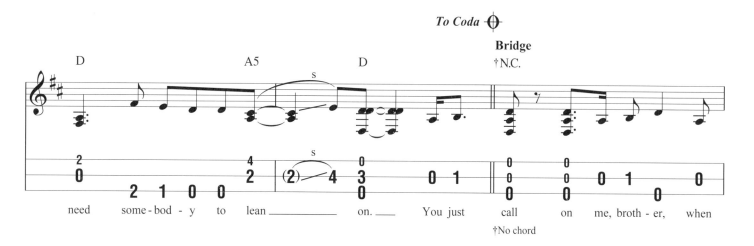

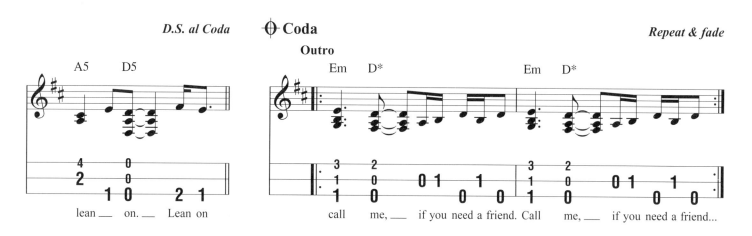

Love Me Tender

Words and Music by Elvis Presley and Vera Matson

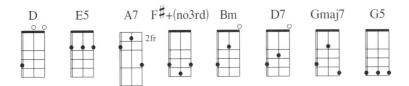

D-A-d tuning
Key: D Major
(Requires 1+ fret)

Verse
Moderately slow

Love me ten - der, love me sweet, nev - er let me go.

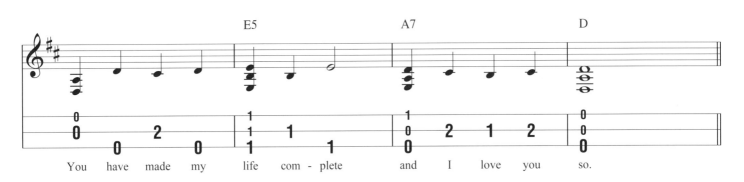

You have made my life com - plete and I love you so.

Chorus

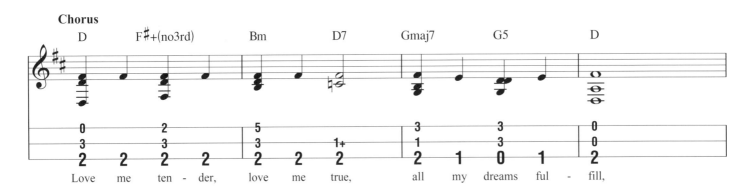

Love me ten - der, love me true, all my dreams ful - fill,

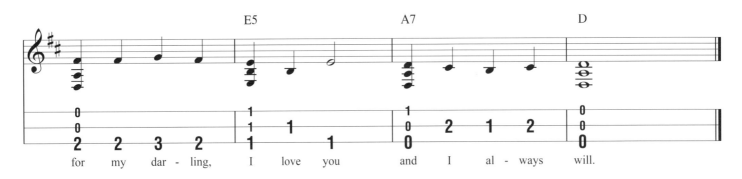

for my dar - ling, I love you and I al - ways will.

Mama Don't 'Low

American Folk Song

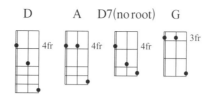

D-A-d tuning
Key: D Major

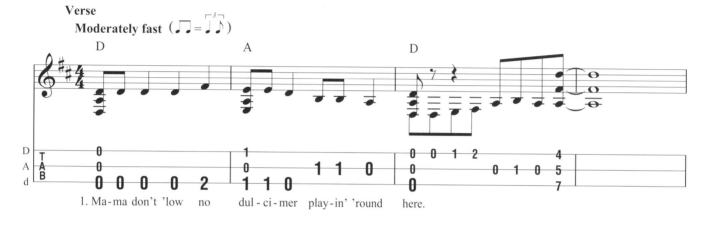

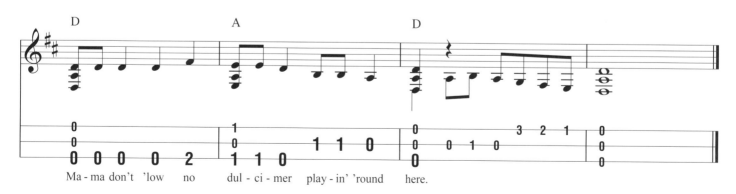

Michael Row the Boat Ashore

Traditional Folksong

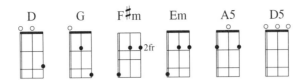

D-A-d tuning
Key: D Major

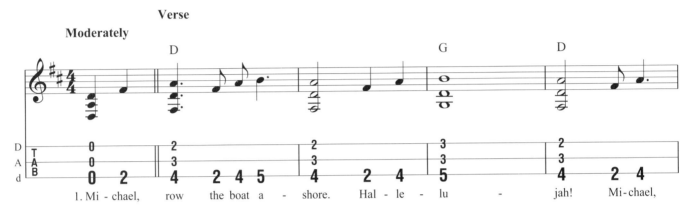

Verse

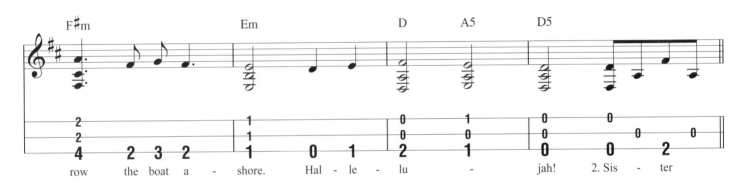

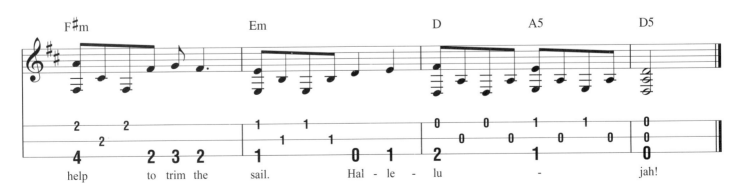

My Girl

Words and Music by Smokey Robinson and Ronald White

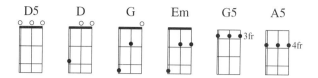

D-A-d tuning
Key: D Major

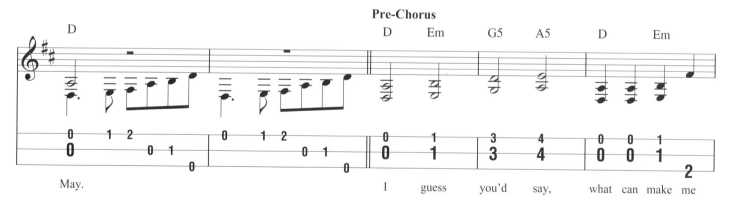

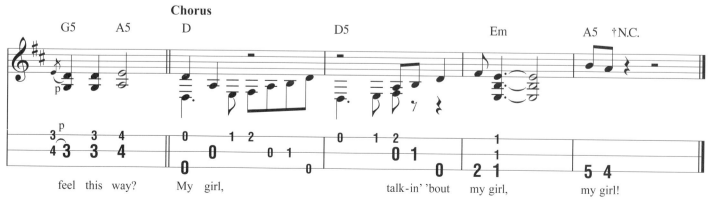

Oh, Pretty Woman

Words and Music by Roy Orbison and Bill Dees

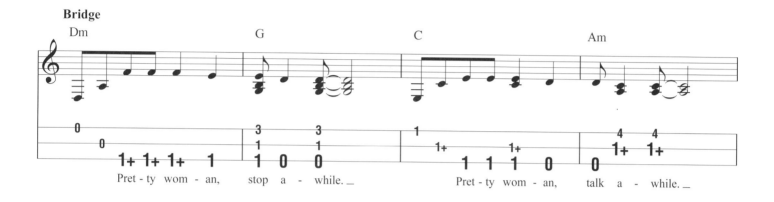

truth. No one could look as good __ as you. Mer-cy. 2. Pret-ty

be. Are you as lone-ly just __ like me.

Bridge

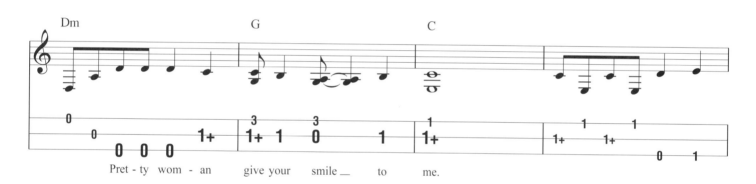

Pret - ty wom - an, stop a - while. __ Pret - ty wom - an, talk a - while. __

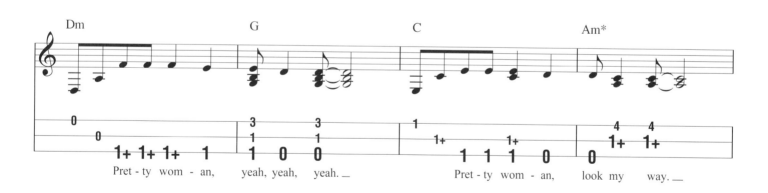

Pret - ty wom - an give your smile __ to me.

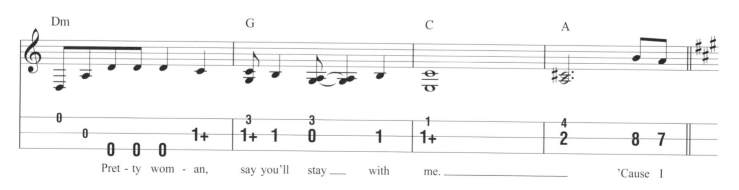

Pret - ty wom - an, yeah, yeah, yeah. __ Pret - ty wom - an, look my way. __

Pret - ty wom - an, say you'll stay __ with me. _____ 'Cause I

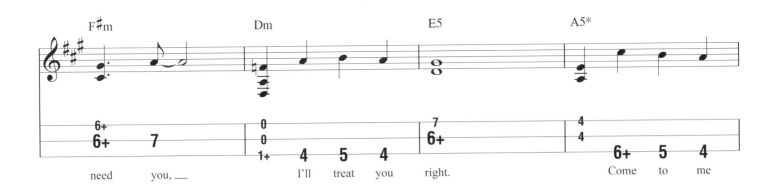

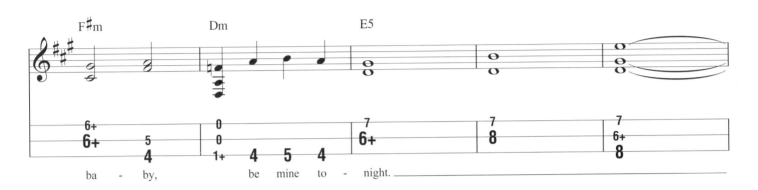

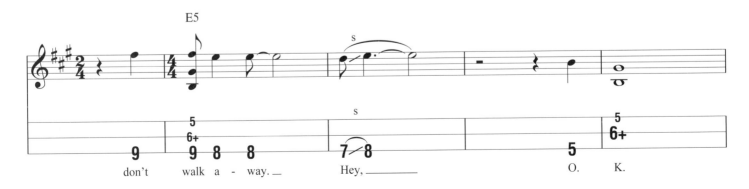

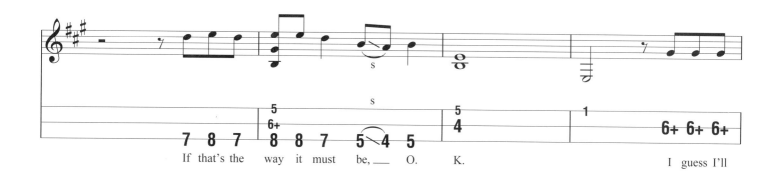

If that's the way it must be,— O. K. I guess I'll

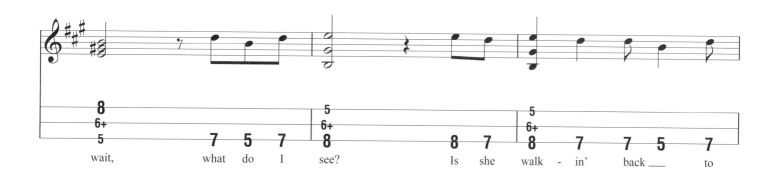

go on home,— it's late. There'll be to - mor - row night,— but

wait, what do I see? Is she walk - in' back — to

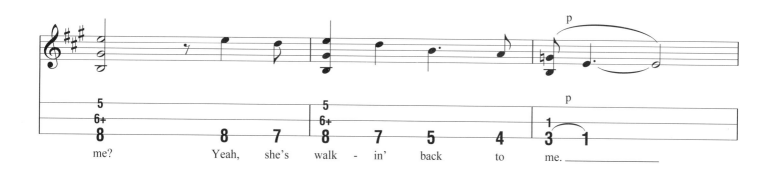

me? Yeah, she's walk - in' back to me. _____

A5*   †N.C.

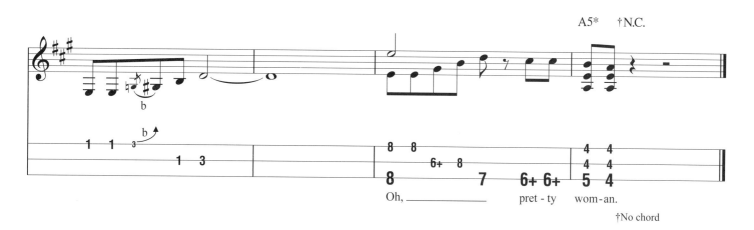

Oh, _____ pret - ty wom-an.

†No chord

The Red River Valley

Traditional American Cowboy Song

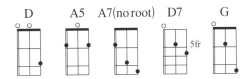

D-A-d tuning
Key: D Major

Verse

Moderately

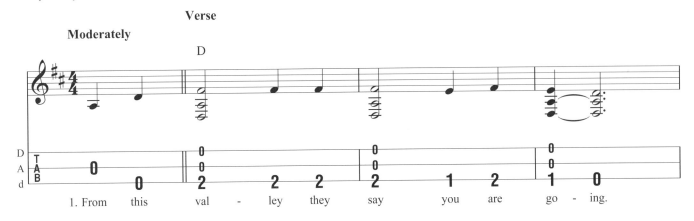

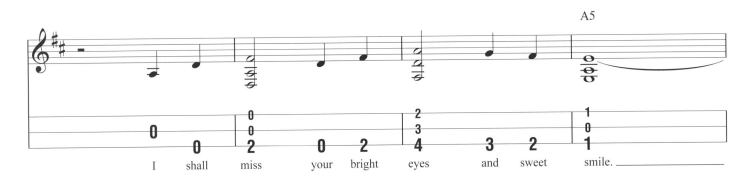

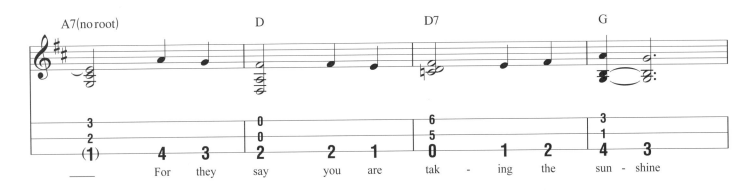

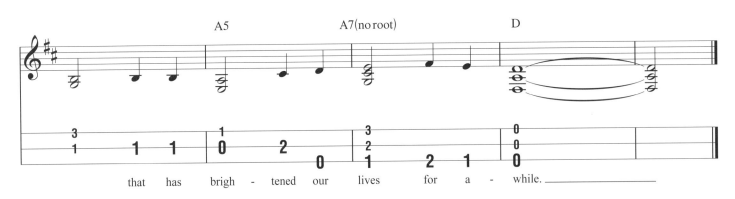

One Tin Soldier

from BILLY JACK

Words and Music by Dennis Lambert and Brian Potter

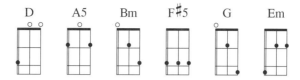

D-A-d tuning
Key: D Major

Intro
Moderately

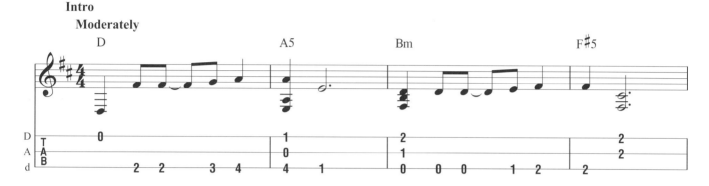

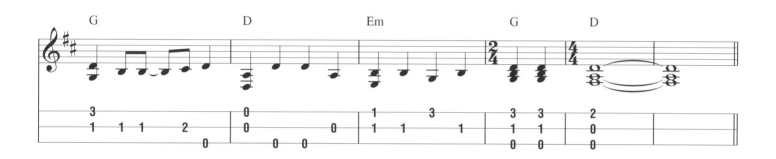

Verse

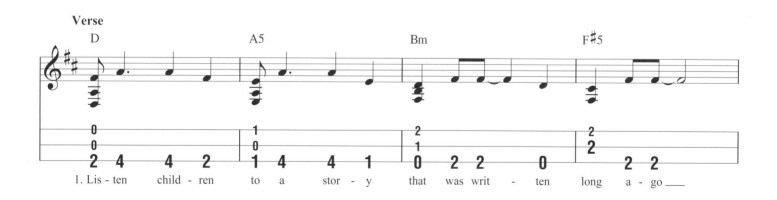

1. Lis - ten child - ren to a stor - y that was writ - ten long a - go ___

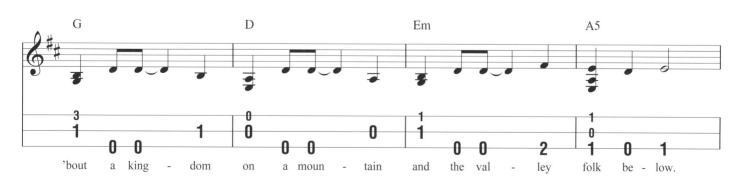

'bout a king - dom on a moun - tain and the val - ley folk be - low.

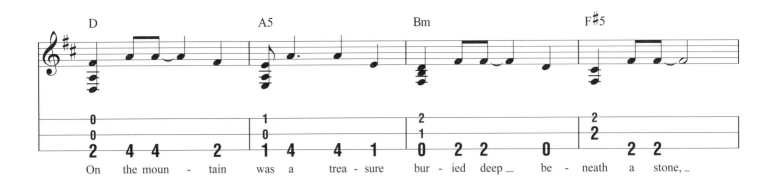

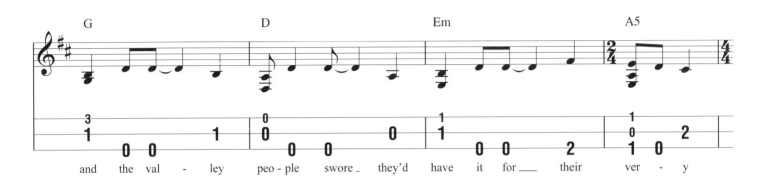

Chorus

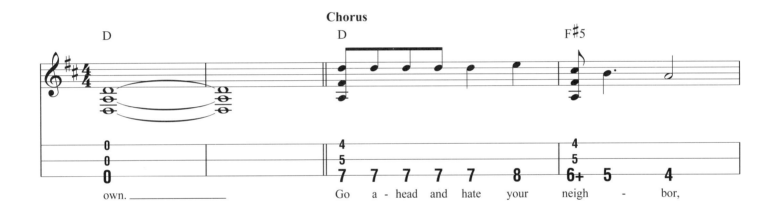

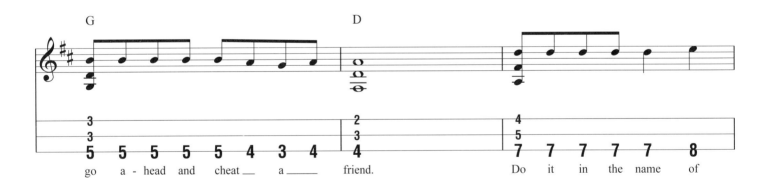

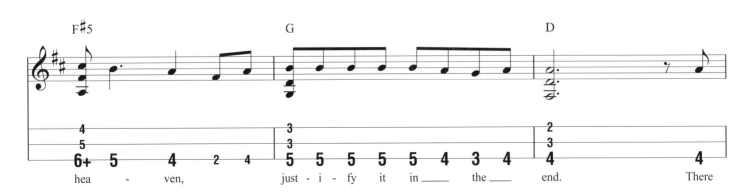

won't be an - y trum - pets blow - in' come the judg - ment

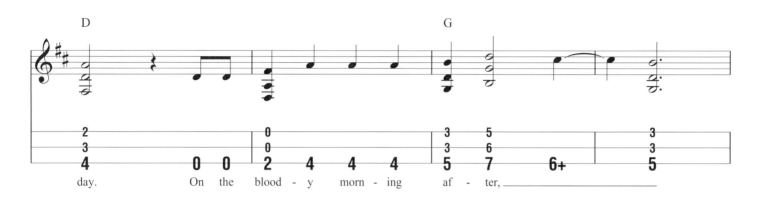

day. On the blood - y morn - ing af - ter,_____

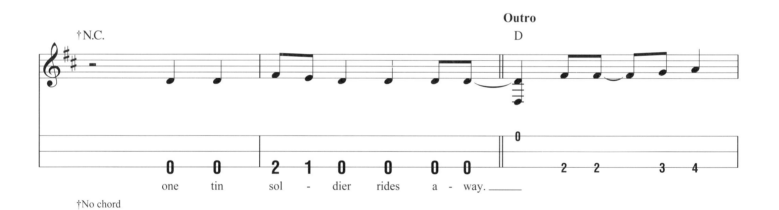

†N.C.

Outro

one tin sol - dier rides a - way._____

†No chord

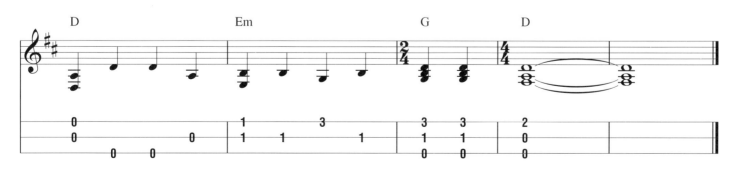

Over the Rainbow

from THE WIZARD OF OZ
Music by Harold Arlen
Lyric by E.Y. "Yip" Harburg

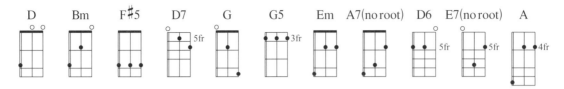

D-A-d tuning
Key: D Major

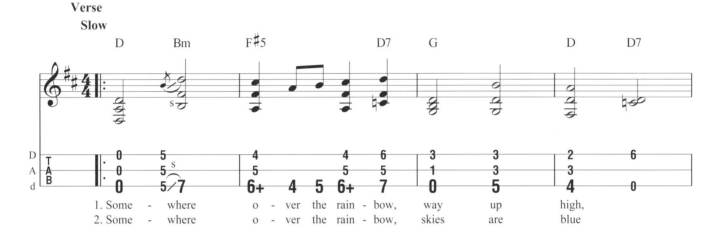

1. Some - where o - ver the rain - bow, way up high,
2. Some - where o - ver the rain - bow, skies are blue

there's a land that I heard of once in a lul - la - by.
and the dreams that you dare to dream real - ly do come

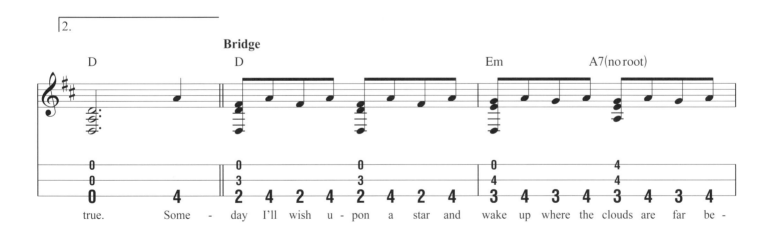

true. Some - day I'll wish u - pon a star and wake up where the clouds are far be -

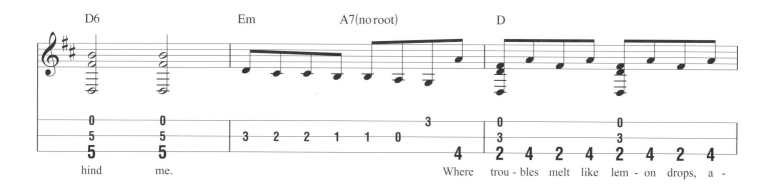

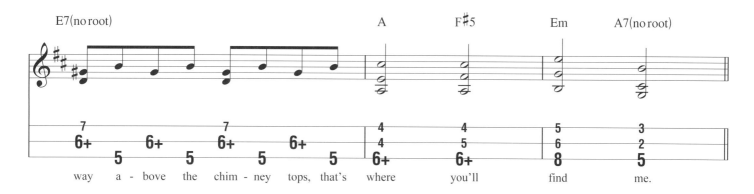

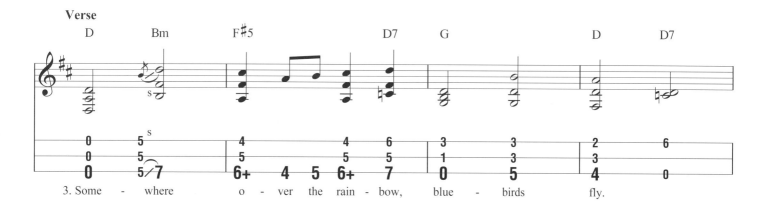

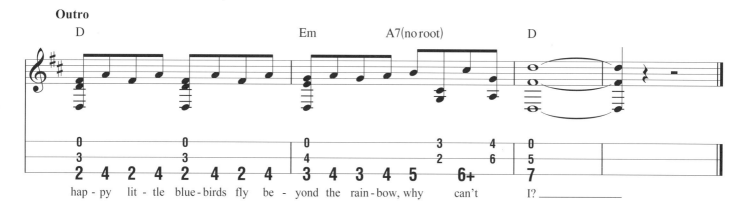

Peaceful Easy Feeling

Words and Music by Jack Tempchin

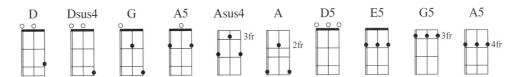

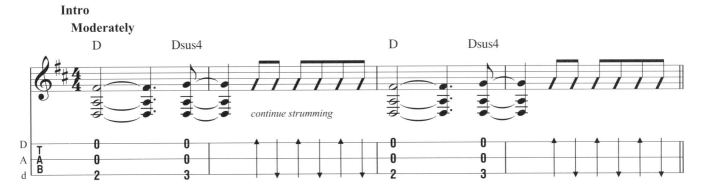

D-A-d tuning
Key: D Major

Intro
Moderately

continue strumming

Verse

1. I like the way your spark-ling ear-ring lay
2. And I found out a long time a-go

a - gainst your skin so brown.
what a wom-an can do to your soul.

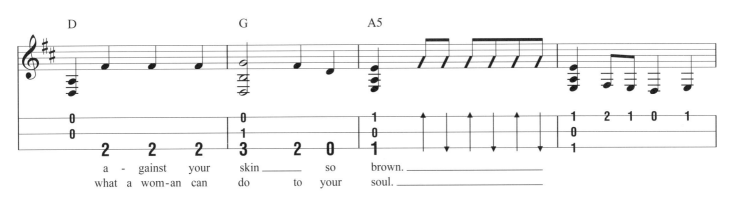

And I want to sleep with you in the de-sert to-night
Aw, but she can't take you an-y-way.

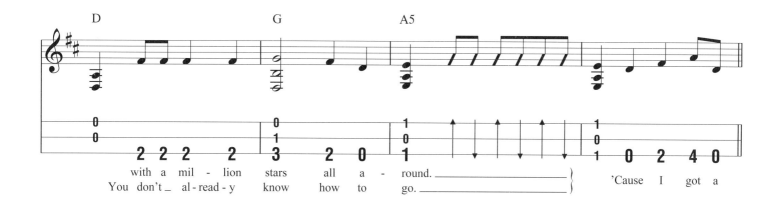

with a mil - lion stars all a - round. _____ } 'Cause I got a
You don't _ al - read - y know how to go. _____ }

Chorus

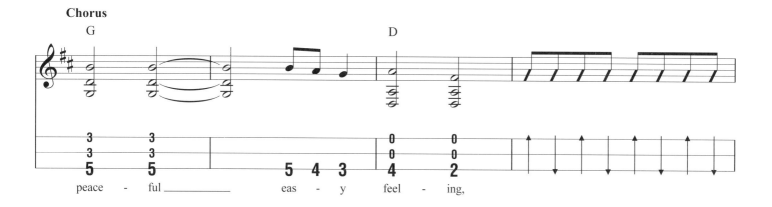

peace - ful _____ eas - y feel - ing,

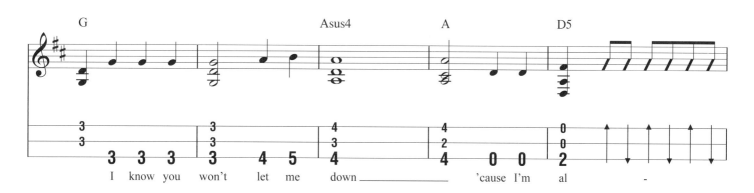

I know you won't let me down _____ 'cause I'm al -

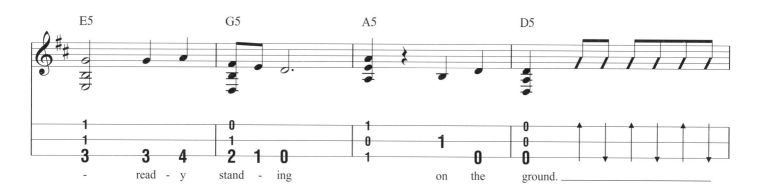

- read - y stand - ing on the ground. _____

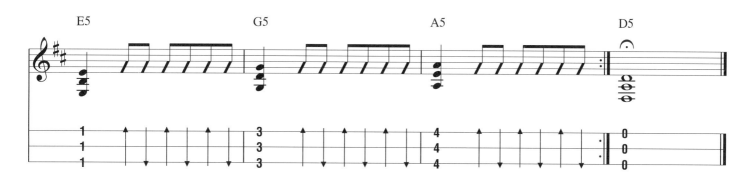

Proud Mary

Words and Music by John Fogerty

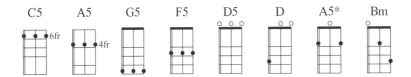

D-A-d tuning
Key: D Major
(Requires 1+ fret)

Intro
Moderately

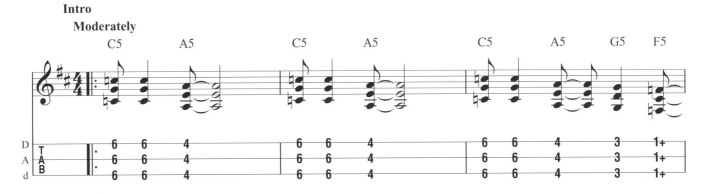

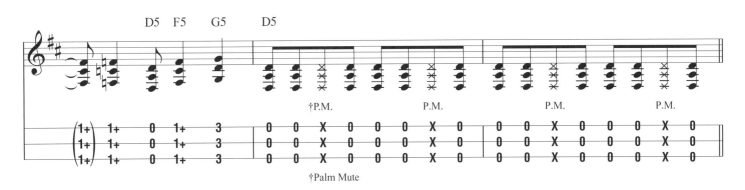

†Palm Mute

Verse

1. Left a good job ___ in the cit - y, ___ work - in' for the man ev' - ry
2. Cleaned a lot of plates in Mem - phis, ___ pumped a lot of pain in

night and day. ___ And I nev - er lost one min - ute of sleep - in',
New Or - leans. ___ But I nev - er saw the good side of the cit - y

Ring of Fire

Words and Music by Merle Kilgore and June Carter

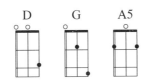

D   G   A5

D-A-d tuning
Key: D Major

Intro
Moderately

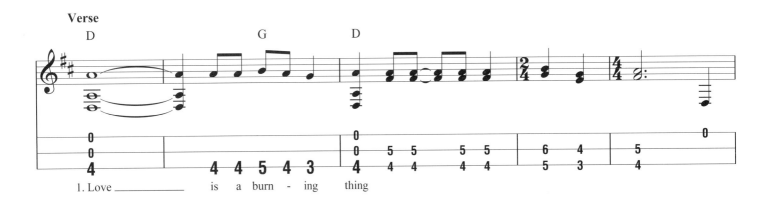

Verse

1. Love _____ is a burn - ing thing

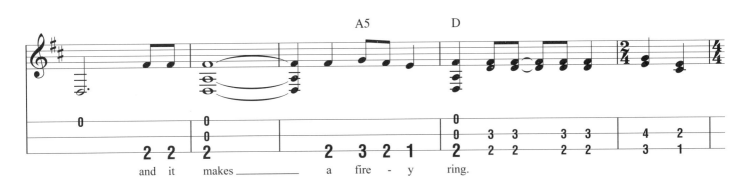

and it makes _____ a fire - y ring.

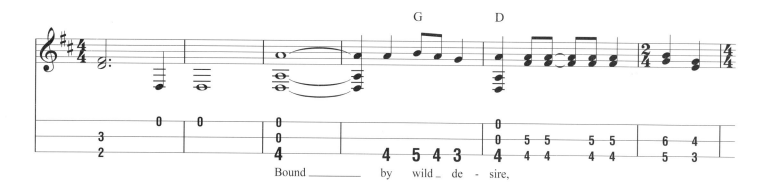

Bound _____ by wild _ de - sire,

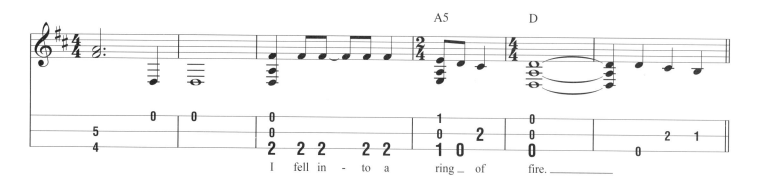

I fell in - to a ring _ of fire. _____

Chorus

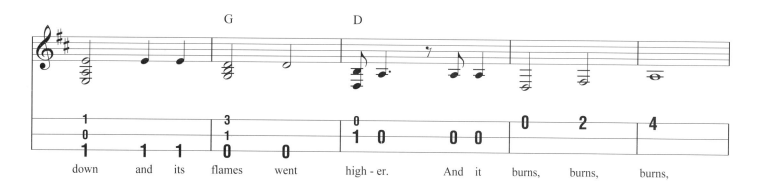

I fell in - to a burn - ing ring _ of fire. _ I went down, down,

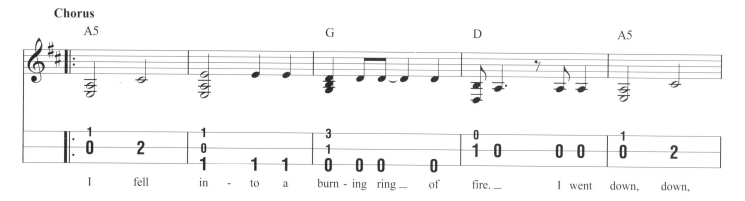

down and its flames went high - er. And it burns, burns, burns,

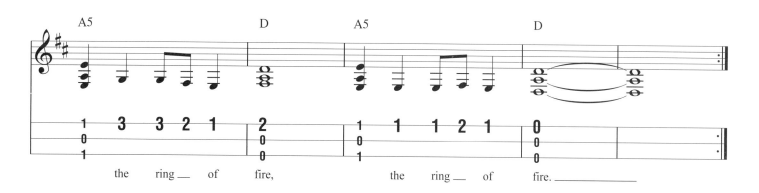

the ring _ of fire, the ring _ of fire. _____

Take Me Home, Country Roads

Words and Music by John Denver, Bill Danoff and Taffy Nivert

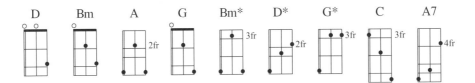

D-A-d tuning
Key: D Major

Intro
Moderately fast

Verse

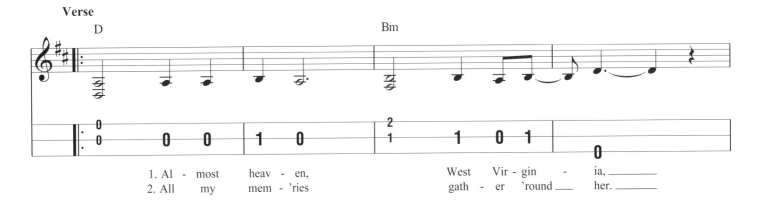

1. Al - most heav - en, West Vir - gin - ia, _____
2. All my mem - 'ries gath - er 'round _____ her. _____

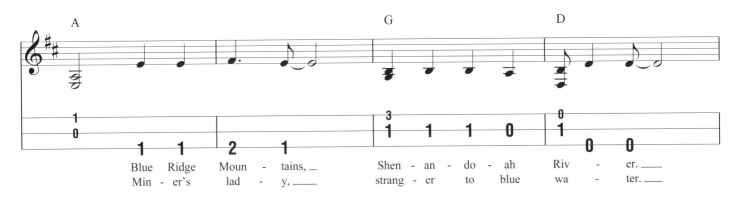

Blue Ridge Moun - tains, ___ Shen - an - do - ah Riv - er. ___
Min - er's lad - y, _____ strang - er to blue wa - ter. ___

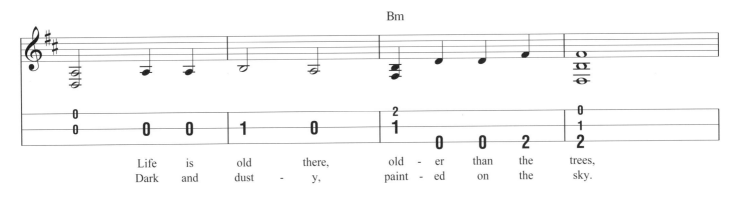

Life is old there, old - er than the trees,
Dark and dust - y, paint - ed on the sky.

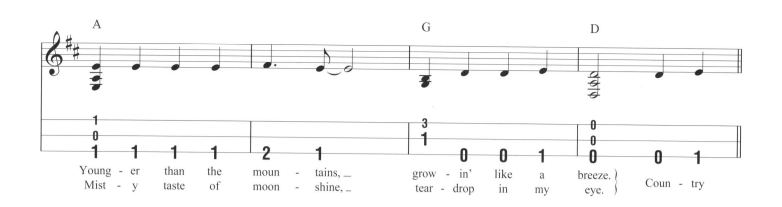

Young - er than the moun - tains, __ grow - in' like a breeze. }
Mist - y taste of moon - shine, __ tear - drop in my eye. } Coun - try

𝄋 Chorus

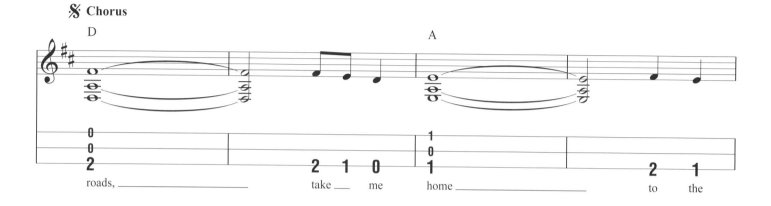

roads, __ take me home __ to the

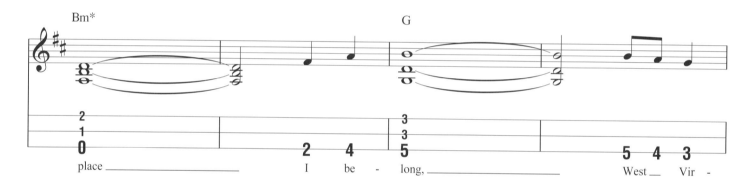

place __ I be - long, __ West __ Vir -

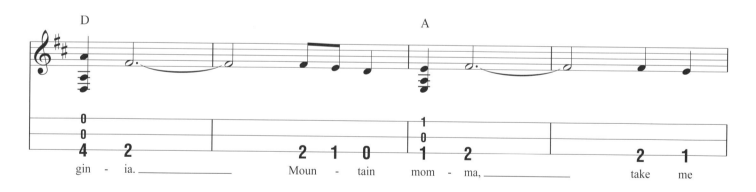

gin - ia. __ Moun - tain mom - ma, __ take me

3rd time, to Coda ⊕ 1. 2.

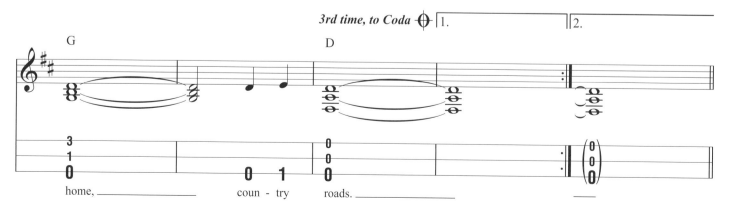

home, __ coun - try roads. __

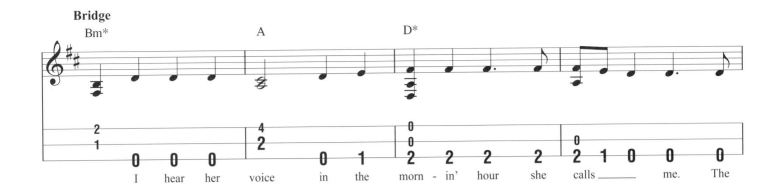

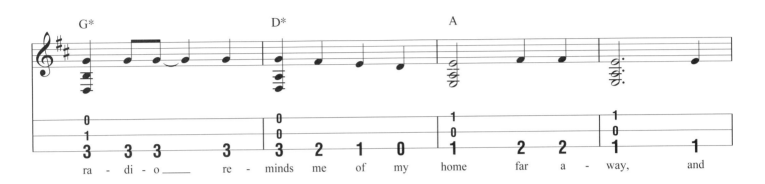

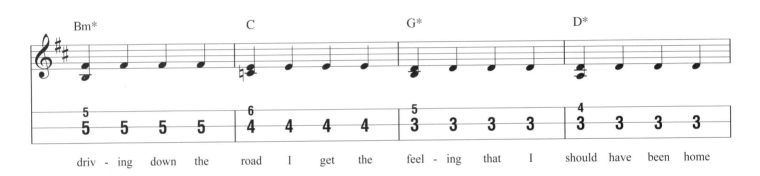

D.S. al Coda   ⊕ **Coda**

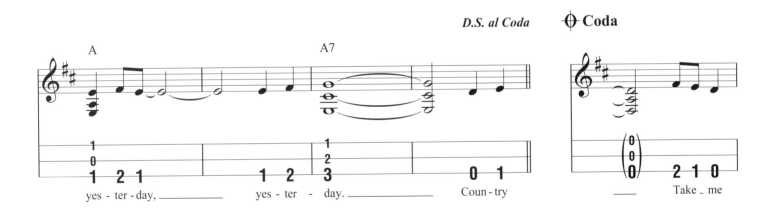

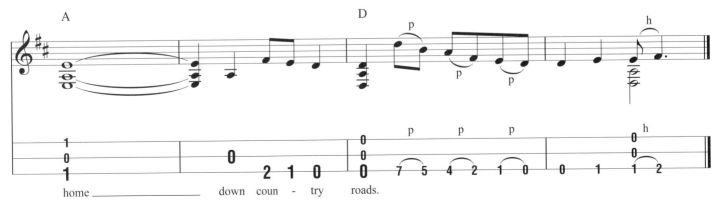

Shenandoah

American Folksong

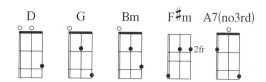

D-A-d tuning
Key: D Major

Verse

Slow

1. Oh, Shen - an - doah, ___ I long to hear you. A -

way, you roll - in' riv - er. ___ Oh, Shen - an - doah, ___ I long to hear you. A -

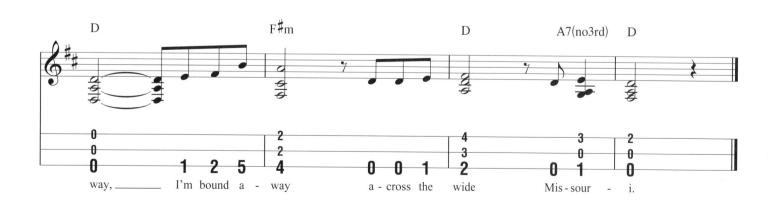

way, ___ I'm bound a - way a - cross the wide Mis - sour - i.

This Land Is Your Land

Words and Music by Woody Guthrie

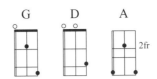

D-A-d tuning
Key: D Major

Verse

Fast, in 2

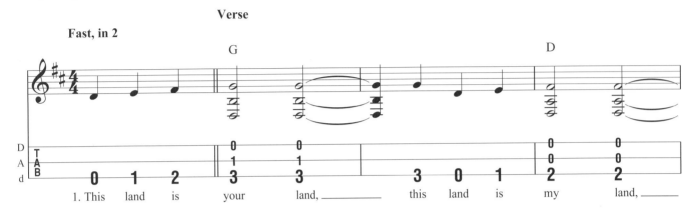

This Little Light of Mine

Traditional

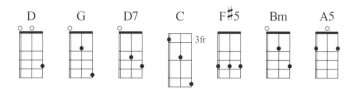

D-A-d tuning
Key: D Major
(Requires 1+ fret)

Verse
Moderately, in 2

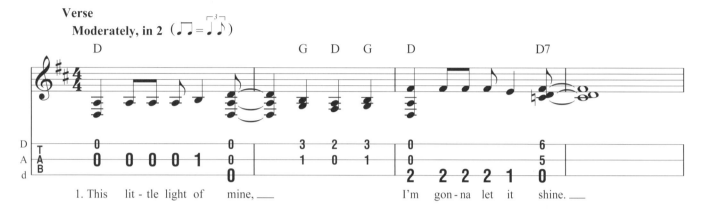

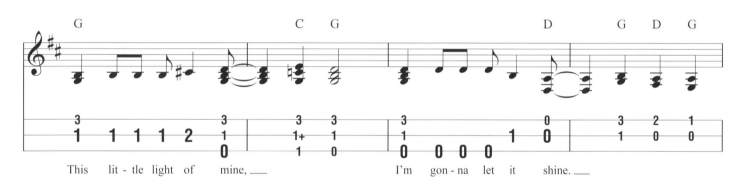

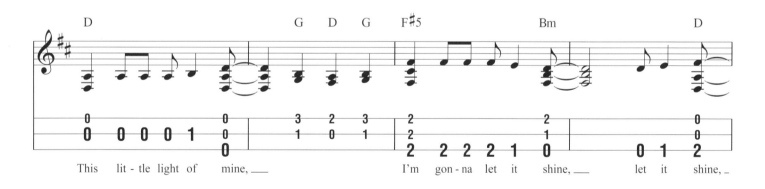

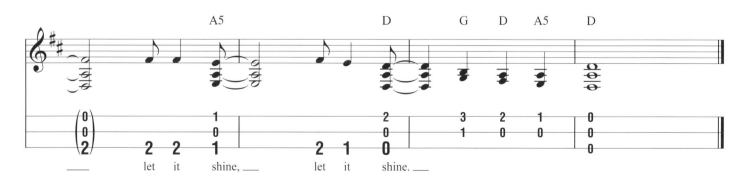

Time After Time

Words and Music by Cyndi Lauper and Rob Hyman

Time in a Bottle

Words and Music by Jim Croce

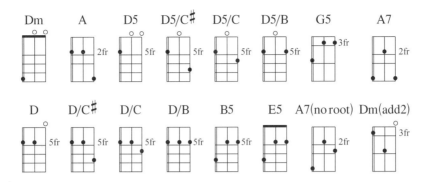

D-A-C tuning
Keys: D minor & D Major

Intro

Moderately

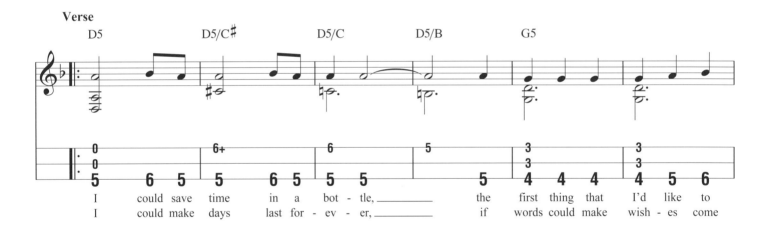

1. If

Verse

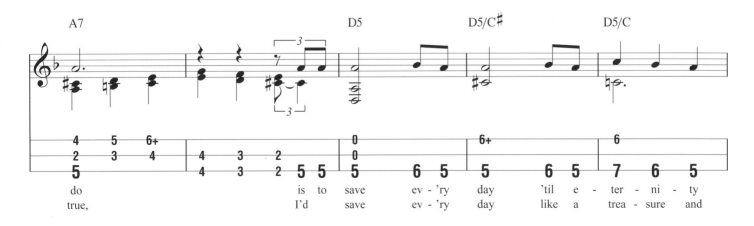

I could save time in a bot - tle, ___ the first thing that I'd like to
I could make days last for - ev - er, ___ if words could make wish - es come

do   is   to   save   ev - 'ry   day   'til e - ter - ni - ty
true,   I'd   save   ev - 'ry   day   like a   trea - sure and

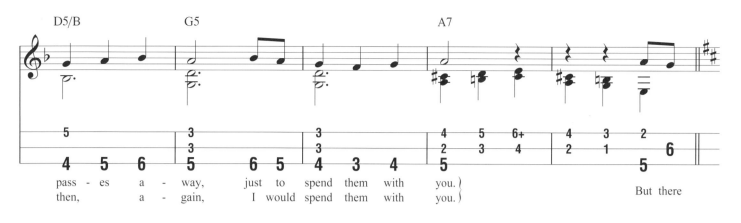

passes a way, just to spend them with you.)
then, a - gain, I would spend them with you.)   But there

Chorus

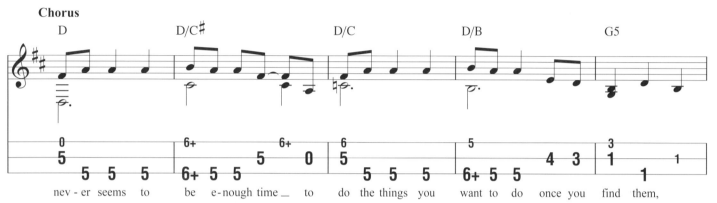

nev - er seems to be e-nough time __ to do the things you want to do once you find them,

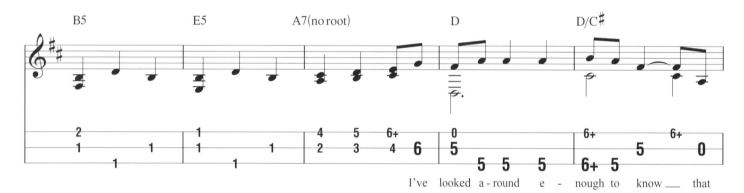

I've looked a - round e - nough to know __ that

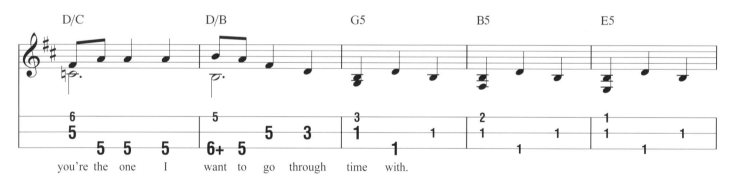

you're the one I want to go through time with.

1.   2.

Outro

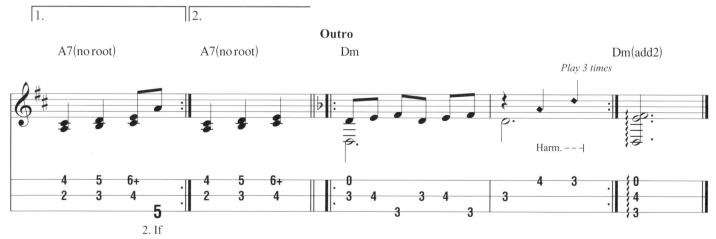

Play 3 times

Harm. ---

2. If

Ventura Highway

Words and Music by Dewey Bunnell

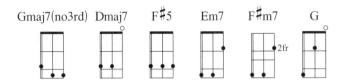

D-A-d tuning
Key: D Major

Intro

Moderately fast

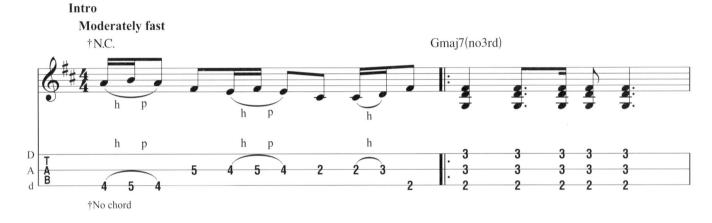

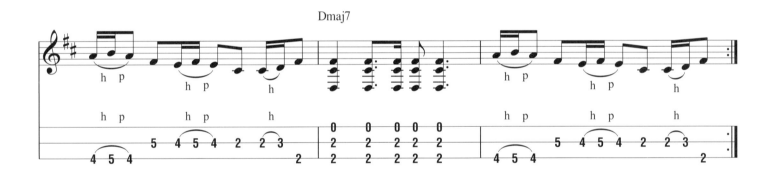

%\ **Verse**

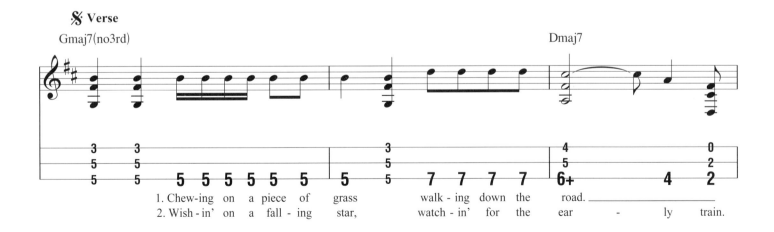

1. Chew-ing on a piece of grass walk-ing down the road.
2. Wish-in' on a fall-ing star, watch-in' for the ear - ly train.

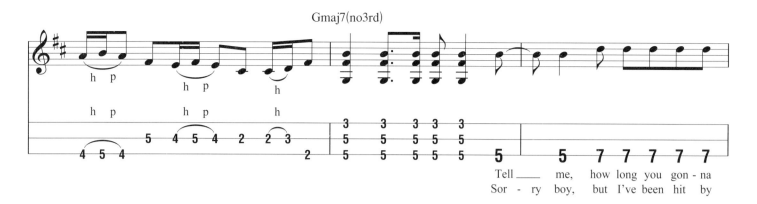

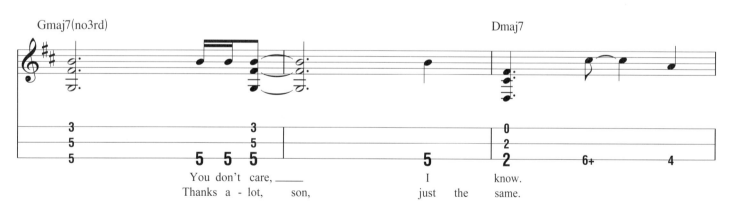

Chorus

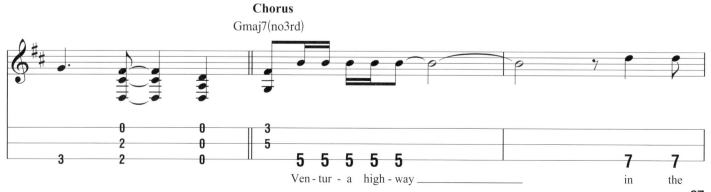

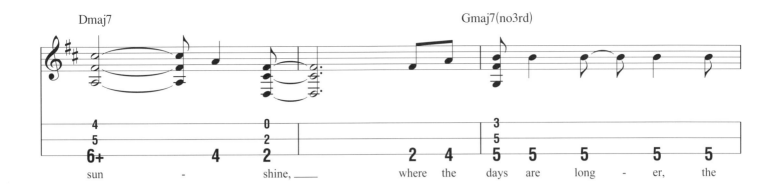

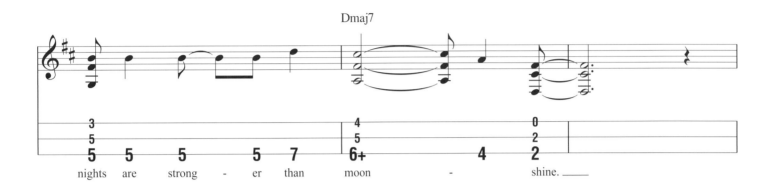

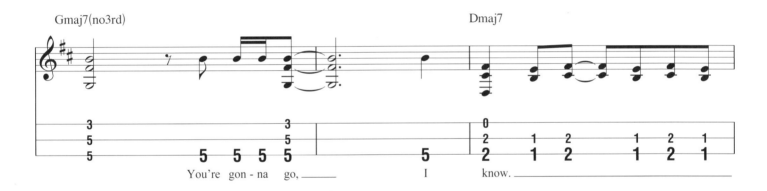

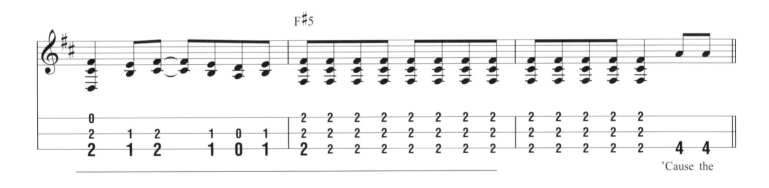

Interlude

To Coda ⊕

D.S. al Coda

⊕ Coda

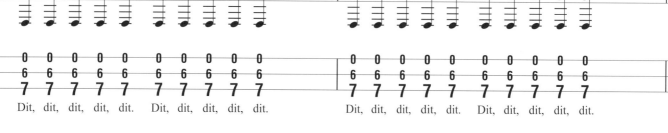

Where've You Been

Words and Music by Don Henry and Jon Vezner

Wonderful Tonight

Words and Music by Eric Clapton

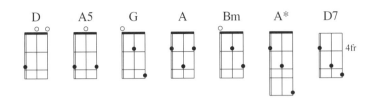

D-A-d tuning
Key: D Major

Intro
Moderately slow

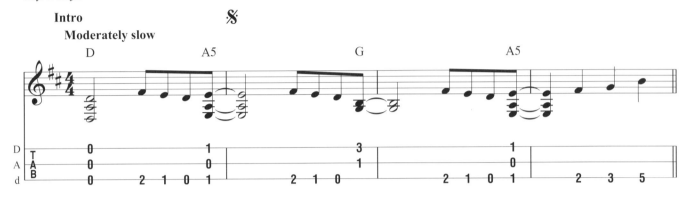

Verse

1., 3. It's late in the eve - ning, _____ she's won-d'ring what clothes _ to wear. _
2. We go to a par - ty, _____ and ev - 'ry - one turns _ to see _

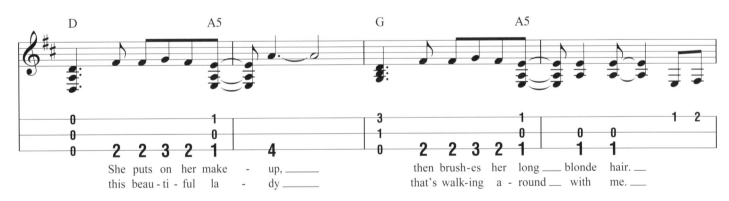

She puts on her make - up, _____ then brush-es her long _ blonde hair. _
this beau-ti - ful la - dy _____ that's walk-ing a - round _ with me. _

And then she'll ask _____ me, _____ "Do I look all right?" And I say,
And then she asked _____ me, _____ "Do you feel all right?" And I say,

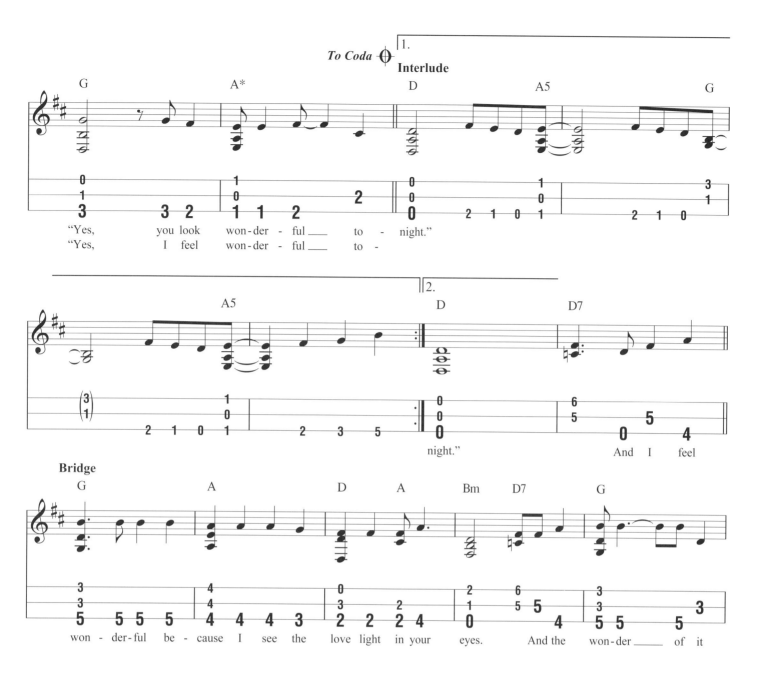

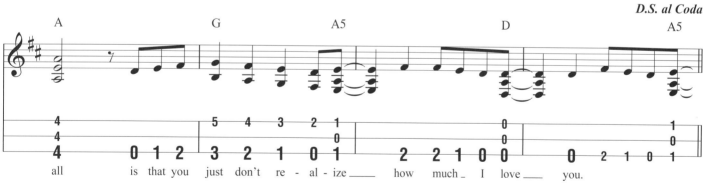

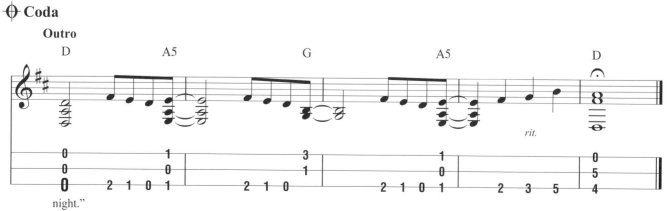

What a Wonderful World

Words and Music by George David Weiss and Bob Thiele

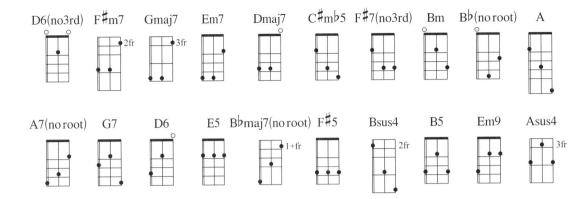

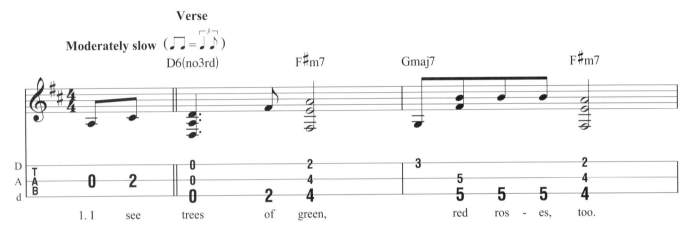

D-A-d tuning
Key: D Major
(Requires 1+ fret)

Verse

Moderately slow

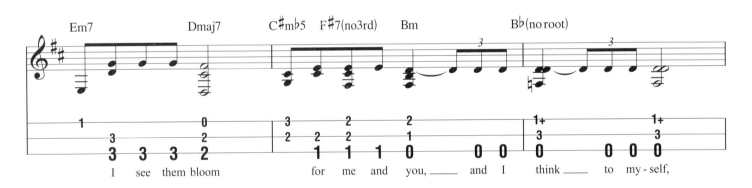

1. I see trees of green, red ros - es, too. I see them bloom for me and you, and I think to my - self,

what a won - der - ful world. 2. I see

Verse

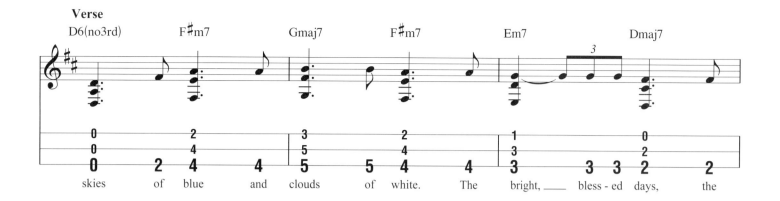

skies of blue and clouds of white. The bright, ____ bless - ed days, the

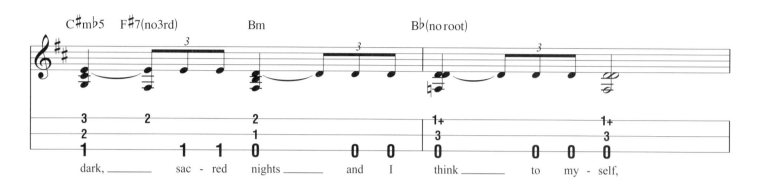

dark, _____ sac - red nights _____ and I think _____ to my - self,

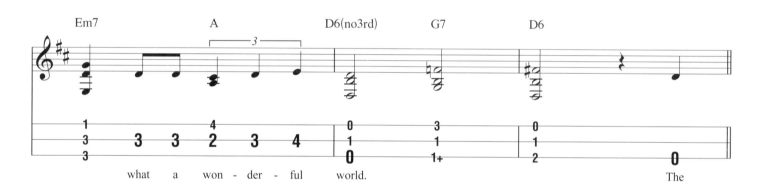

what a won - der - ful world. The

Bridge

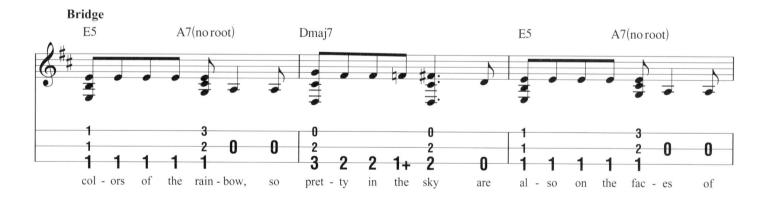

col - ors of the rain - bow, so pret - ty in the sky are al - so on the fac - es of

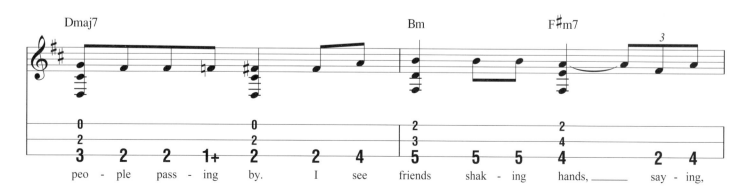

peo - ple pass - ing by. I see friends shak - ing hands, _____ say - ing,

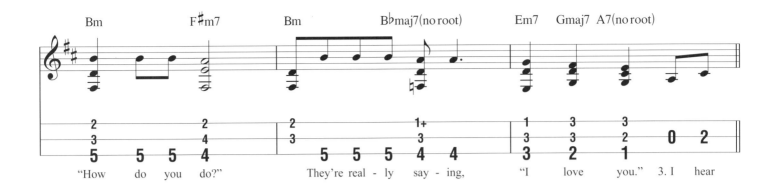

"How do you do?" They're real - ly say - ing, "I love you." 3. I hear

Verse

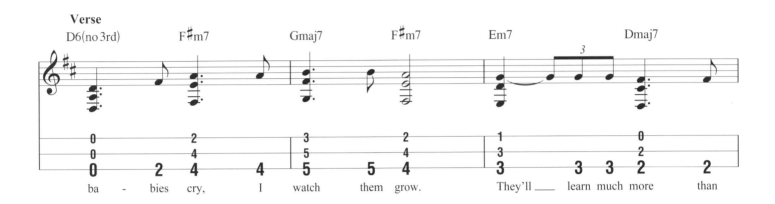

ba - bies cry, I watch them grow. They'll ___ learn much more than

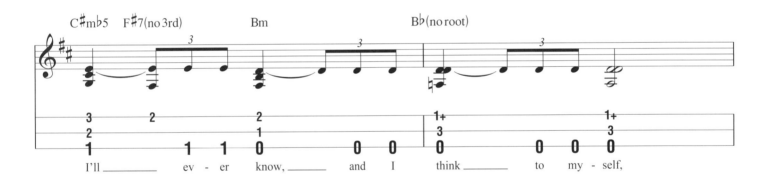

I'll _____ ev - er know, _____ and I think _____ to my - self,

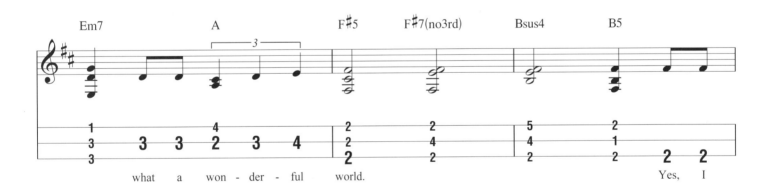

what a won - der - ful world. Yes, I

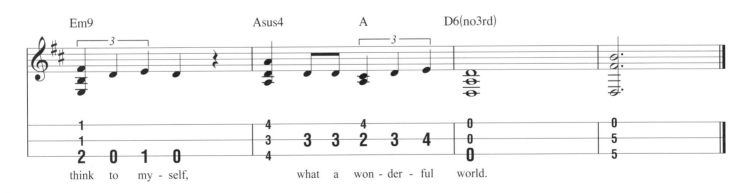

think to my - self, what a won - der - ful world.

You've Got a Friend

Words and Music by Carole King

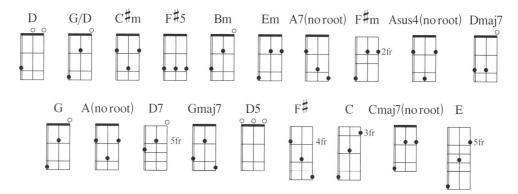

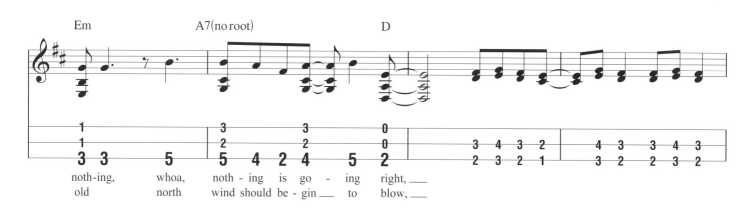

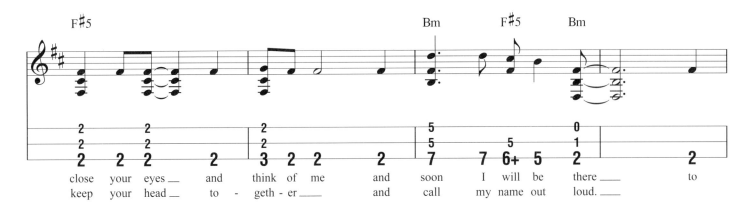

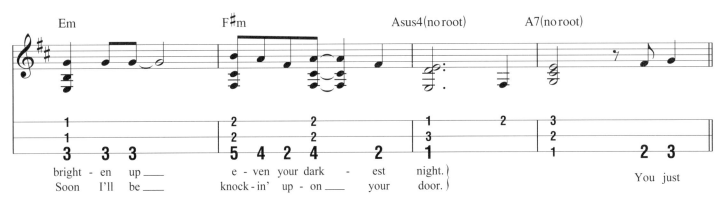

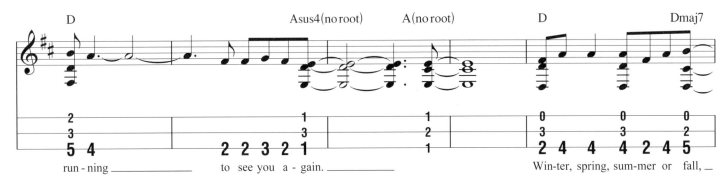

Your Song

Words and Music by Elton John and Bernie Taupin

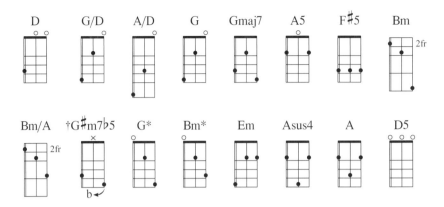

D-A-d tuning
Key: D Major
(Requires 1+ fret)

Intro
Moderately fast

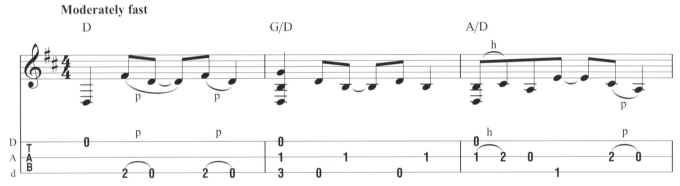

Verse

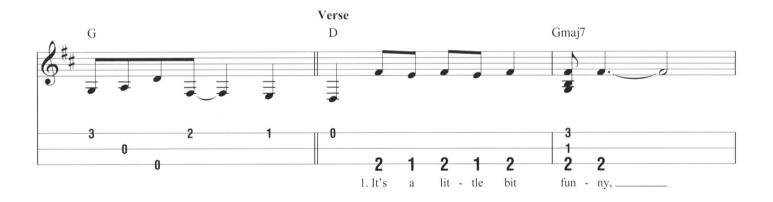

1. It's a lit-tle bit fun-ny, _____

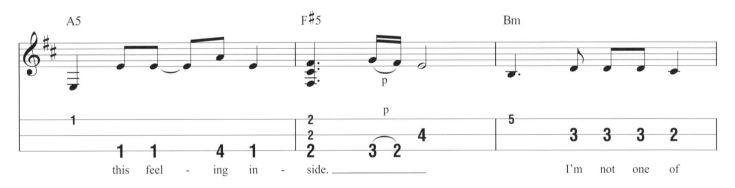

this feel-ing in-side. _____ I'm not one of

†G#m7♭5 reflects the implied harmony. Bend G note to G#

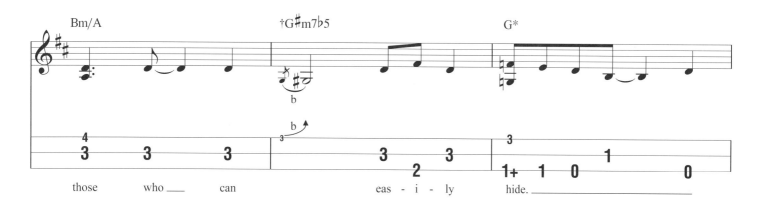

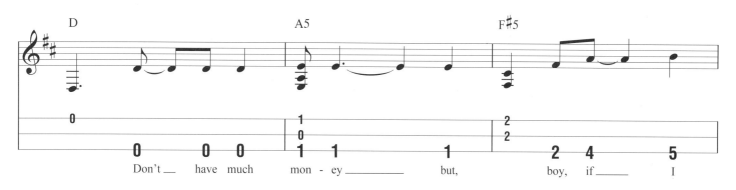

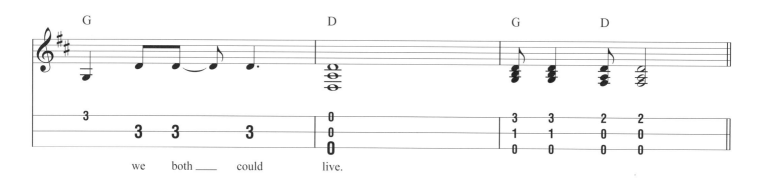

Chorus

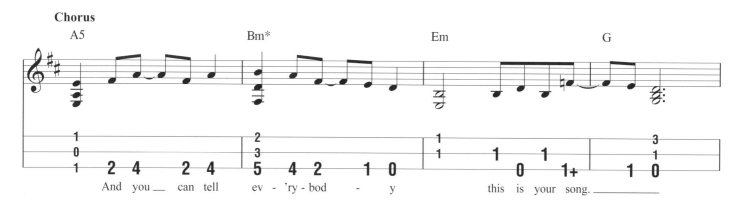

Learn to Play Today
with folk music instruction from Hal Leonard

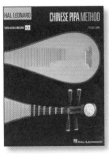

MOUNTAIN DULCIMER NOTATION LEGEND

Mountain dulcimer music can be notated three different ways: with *chord diagrams*, on a *musical staff*, and in *tablature*.

CHORD DIAGRAMS represent a small portion of the fretboard: the vertical lines represent the strings and the horizontal lines represent the frets. Most diagrams will have a bold horizontal line above that represents the nut. Solid dots indicate the finger locations of fretted notes, while open circles above the strings indicate open strings that are included in the chord. A string which should not be played will have an "x" above the grid. If the chord diagram does not pertain to the lowest portion of the fretboard, a fret indication will be placed to the right of the diagram. These chord diagrams are meant for general accompaniment and should be strummed. Chord names followed by an asterisk (*) indicate a second version of a chord already used.

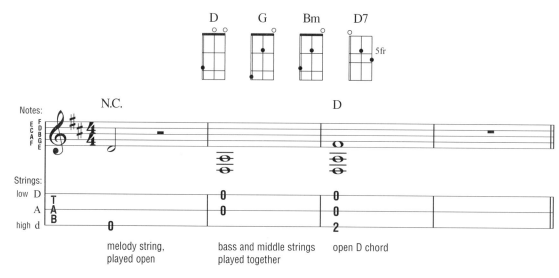

melody string, played open

bass and middle strings played together

open D chord

THE MUSICAL STAFF shows pitches and rhythms and is divided by bar lines into measures. Pitches are named after the first seven letters of the alphabet.

TABLATURE graphically represents the dulcimer fretboard. Each of the three horizontal lines represents the strings—the bottom line represents the double melody string—and each number represents a fret.

Definitions for Special Mountain Dulcimer Notation

HAMMER-ON: Strike the first (lower) note with one finger, then sound the higher note (on the same string) with another finger by fretting it without picking.

PULL-OFF: Place both fingers on the notes to be sounded. Strike the first note and without picking, pull the finger off to sound the second (lower) note.

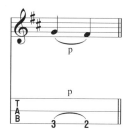

SLIDE: Strike the first note and then slide the same fret-hand finger up or down to the second note. The second not is not struck.

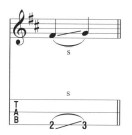

BEND: Strike the first note and, while depressing the string, pull the string causing the pitch to be raised to the second note.

GRACE NOTE BEND: The technique is identical to a bend, but the string is pulled immediately after being struck. The tiny grace note has not rhythmic time value.

HARMONICS: Strike the note while the fret-hand finger lightly touches the string directly over the fret indicated.

STRUM: Strike the notes simultaneously and continue in the rhythm indicated by the rhythm slashes and arrows.

PALM MUTE: Like the strum, strike the strings simultaneously but rest the palm of your picking hand on the strings for a percussive effect.

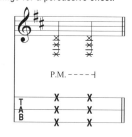

Additional Musical Definitions

p (piano)	• Play quietly.
mp (mezzo-piano)	• Play moderately quiet.
mf (mezzo-forte)	• Play moderately loud.
f (forte)	• Play loudly.
cont. rhy. sim.	• Continue strumming in similar rhythm.
N.C. *(no chord)*	• Don't strum until the next chord symbol. Chord symbols in parentheses reflect implied harmony.
D.S. al Coda	• Go back to the sign (𝄋), then play until the measure marked *"To Coda"*, then skip to the section labeled **"Coda."**
D.C. al Coda	• Go back to the beginning then play until the measure marked *"To Coda"*, then skip to the section labeled **"Coda."**
D.S. al Fine	• Go back to the sign (𝄋), then play until the label ***"Fine."***

(staccato) • Play the note or chord short.

rit.
(ritard) • Gradually slow down.

(fermata) • Hold the note or chord for an undetermined amount of time.

• Repeat measures between signs.

1. 2.
• When a repeated section has different endings, play the first ending only the first time and the second ending only the second time.

NOTE: Tablature numbers in parentheses mean:
1. The note is being sustained over a system (note in standard notation is tied), or
2. The note is sustained, but a new articulation (such as a hammer-on, pull-off or slide) begins.